Oxford Shakespeare Topics

Shakespeare and Disability Studies

OXFORD SHAKESPEARE TOPICS

Published and forthcoming titles include:

David Bevington, *Shakespeare and Biography*
Colin Burrow, *Shakespeare and Classical Antiquity*
Michael Caines, *Shakespeare and the Eighteenth Century*
Lawrence Danson, *Shakespeare's Dramatic Genres*
Janette Dillon, *Shakespeare and the Staging of English History*
Paul Edmondson and Stanley Wells, *Shakespeare's Sonnets*
Gabriel Egan, *Shakespeare and Marx*
Andrew Gurr and Mariko Ichikawa, *Staging in Shakespeare's Theatres*
Jonathan Gil Harris, *Shakespeare and Literary Theory*
Russell Jackson, *Shakespeare and the English-speaking Cinema*
John Jowett, *Shakespeare and Text*
Douglas Lanier, *Shakespeare and Modern Popular Culture*
Hester Lees-Jeffries, *Shakespeare and Memory*
Ania Loomba, *Shakespeare, Race, and Colonialism*
Raphael Lyne, *Shakespeare's Late Work*
Russ McDonald, *Shakespeare and the Arts of Language*
Steven Marx, *Shakespeare and the Bible*
Robert S. Miola, *Shakespeare's Reading*
Marianne Novy, *Shakespeare and Outsiders*
Phyllis Rackin, *Shakespeare and Women*
Catherine Richardson, *Shakespeare and Material Culture*
Ducan Salkeld, *Shakespeare and London*
Stuart Sillars, *Shakespeare and the Victorians*
Bruce R. Smith, *Shakespeare and Masculinity*
Zdenek Stríbrny, *Shakespeare and Eastern Europe*
Michael Taylor, *Shakespeare Criticism in the Twentieth Century*
Alden T. Vaughan and Virginia Mason Vaughan, *Shakespeare in America*
Stanley Wells, ed., *Shakespeare in the Theatre: An Anthology of Criticism*
Martin Wiggins, *Shakespeare and the Drama of his Time*

Oxford Shakespeare Topics

GENERAL EDITORS: LENA COWEN ORLIN, PETER HOLLAND, AND STANLEY WELLS

Shakespeare and Disability Studies

SONYA FREEMAN LOFTIS

OXFORD
UNIVERSITY PRESS

Great Clarendon Street, Oxford, OX2 6DP,
United Kingdom

Oxford University Press is a department of the University of Oxford. It furthers the University's objective of excellence in research, scholarship, and education by publishing worldwide. Oxford is a registered trade mark of Oxford University Press in the UK and in certain other countries

First Edition published in 2021

Published in the United States of America by Oxford University Press
198 Madison Avenue, New York, NY 10016, United States of America

British Library Cataloguing in Publication Data
Data available

Library of Congress Control Number: 2020947779

ISBN 978–0–19–886453–0 (hbk.)
ISBN 978–0–19–886454–7 (pbk.)

For Finneas and Delia

Acknowledgements

I'm grateful to the editors of the Oxford Shakespeare Topics Series, Lena Cowen Orlin, Peter Holland, and Stanley Wells, as well as to Ellie Collins at Oxford University Press, for encouragement and support. Thank you to those who commented on chapters in progress, among them Fran Teague, Linda Zatlin, Lisa Ulevich, Alison Ligon, Allison Kellar, and Cordaro Shaw. Thank you to David Bellwood (Shakespeare's Globe), Josefa MacKinnon (Royal Shakespeare Company), and Julie Simon (Oregon Shakespeare Festival), who generously gave their time for Skype interviews: I'm grateful for their contribution to this book and to the work of creating access to theatre for people with disabilities. Portions of Chapter 3 first appeared as "Autistic Culture, Shakespeare Therapy and the Hunter Heartbeat Method" in *Shakespeare Survey* 72 (ed. Emma Smith, 2019, pp. 256–67) and are reprinted here with the permission of Cambridge University Press through PLSclear. Thank you to my research assistants, Jabril Lovelady and Artimus Cunningham: Jabril was always patient with me, and Artimus learned first-hand about working with and through crip time. Thanks to the friends who helped me to think through chapters and work through stress, especially Stephanie Frankum Lewis, Andera Joy Richardson, and Alice Sheppard. Finally, thank you to my amazing husband, Matt Loftis, and my wonderful mother, Susan Freeman, who provided emotional support, childcare, and pep talks.

I'm grateful to my students at Morehouse College, especially the students in my Introduction to Disability Studies classes and my Disability and Race classes during the 2018–20 school years. Many students participated in discussions about the disability issues discussed in this book during class, during office hours, and by email: special thanks to Cordaro Shaw, Steven Anderson, Julian Hemmings, Artimus Cunningham, Jabril Lovelady, and Dale Kight.

Contents

Introduction

Theory, Access, Inclusion

I'm a Shakespearian, and I have a disability. In some situations, I do not need any disability accommodations to engage with Shakespeare's plays. In others, I need so many accommodations that it is difficult to include me. For example, the expectations set for theatregoers (sitting still in a crowded theatre) were not designed for someone with my impairments. Thus, I am a Shakespearian who rarely goes to the theatre. Modern requirements for travel (flying on a plane, staying in a hotel, navigating city streets) were not designed with me in mind either. Thus, I am a Shakespearian who rarely travels to professional conferences, and one who never travels without substantial help. It is difficult for me to navigate to and from and around the campus library—almost everything I read as I was researching this book came to me electronically (via interlibrary loan or Kindle e-book). Because I am a Shakespearian whose experience of disability affects my access to what many people consider to be central to the study of Shakespeare (attending plays, going to lectures, reading in the library), I have a personal investment in the topic of this book: the critical connections between disability studies and Shakespeare studies.

While there are important intersections between these two fields in my own life, the joining of Shakespeare studies and disability studies has seemed like a less intuitive union to some scholars. As an interdisciplinary field of critical inquiry, disability studies grew in tandem with the disability rights movement, and disability studies approaches to literature have increased in popularity since the 1990s. Like feminist theory, critical race theory, and queer theory, disability theory focuses

Shakespeare and Disability Studies. Sonya Freeman Loftis, Oxford University Press (2021).
 DOI: 10.1093/oso/9780198864530.003.0001

on a minority experience of embodiment, examines the ways that this embodiment can be understood as a cultural construct, and investigates the power dynamic between the assumed 'norm' (that which is labelled 'able-bodied') and those who experience the social effects of the minority label. Given the history of discrimination and oppression that people with disabilities have experienced, prioritizing the lived experience of people with disabilities as a source of knowledge is a central tenet of disability studies. Ableist discrimination and assumptions mean that it is all too common for adults with disabilities to be treated as though they were children and for them to be seen as 'incompetent' to speak for themselves or to make their own decisions (this is especially true for those with mental disabilities). Coming in the wake of a modern history in which many people with physical and mental disabilities were institutionalized, their decisions made for them by parents or caregivers, this prioritizing of lived experience as a source of knowledge is encapsulated in the motto of the disability rights movement: 'Nothing about us without us'. Hence, the opening of this book, in which I disclose my own disability, is a common critical manoeuvre in disability studies scholarship—but a more unusual one in Shakespeare studies. A far more traditional field of critical inquiry, Shakespeare criticism more often conveys a sense of the author as a disengaged and disembodied critic who reads the works of Shakespeare from an imagined impersonal viewpoint. Unsurprisingly, most applications of disability theory to Shakespeare follow this 'disembodied Shakespearian' stance, focusing on Renaissance characters that a modern audience might view as disabled rather than examining the lived reality of users of Shakespeare with disabilities. However, this conception of disability as residing within individual literary characters has limited understandings of disability in Shakespeare studies.[1] By theorizing disability vis-à-vis characters, many studies have largely overlooked readers, performers, and audience members who self-identify as disabled. Thus, this book focuses on ways to read Shakespeare through the lens of critical disability theory that work outside of literary character, encouraging users of Shakespeare to consider how Shakespeare (as industry, as high art, as cultural symbol) affects the lived reality of those with disabled bodies and/or minds.

Disability Theory and Shakespeare

Oddly enough, early modern disability studies' central focus on literary characters sometimes leads the field in directions that are not in keeping with the body of scholarship published in disability studies proper; specifically, the focus on an individual body in such criticism is at odds with the larger trajectory of the field, which emphasizes disability as a minority cultural experience. Disability studies reveals disability as a complex and specifically cultural phenomenon. I often find that my able-bodied students have given little thought to this matter: many come into my classes understanding 'disability' as a simple fact of biology (this body and/or mind is different from the able-bodied norm). In other words, most of them are only familiar with the medical model of disability—a world view that sees disability as an individual deficit or problem in need of treatment or cure. Disability theory posits other ways of understanding disability; for example, the social model of disability creates a distinction between 'impairment' and 'disability', defining 'impairment' as the biological fact of difference and 'disability' as the physical and social environment's failure to accommodate impairment. Thus, someone who cannot walk is impaired—but he or she is only disabled when encountering an environment that uses stairs instead of providing wheelchair ramps. In this way, the social model of disability views disability as a social construct: impairment is a biological fact, but through the failure to create accommodating environments that welcome different kinds of bodies and minds, human society creates disability.

My personal experience of disability has taught me that ableist social attitudes and unaccommodating environments create many of the challenges in my life—these difficulties are rarely caused simply by my impairment. If the able-bodied norm is itself a social construct, it is possible to imagine a world in which everyone had my impairments—and, in that world, everything (including theatres and libraries) would be designed so that people with my impairments could easily navigate and use them. Rather than regarding impairment as a pathological state, as the medical model of disability does, the social model of disability regards impairment as a normal form of human diversity. For example, the neurodiversity movement, a subset of the disability rights movement, argues that mental disability (autism, schizophrenia, intellectual disability) is a natural and potentially valuable form of human diversity. From this movement, we gain new terminology for mental disability: a neurodiverse person is someone with a mental disability, while a neurotypical person is someone who does not have a mental disability. Disability studies' emphasis on disability as cultural construct also emphasizes disability *as culture*. Although the medical model regards disability as a 'problem' that resides within individual bodies and minds, disability studies recognizes disability as a fundamentally cultural matter—people with different kinds of disabilities (blind people, autistic people) form cultural groups with their own unique disability subcultures. Ironically, early modern studies that focus on literary character may unintentionally parallel the medical model of disability. By regarding disability as an individual difference that resides within each separate literary character (rather than as a broader social phenomenon that affects readers, audience members, and performers), many of these readings foreground disability as an individual condition that one character/figure has as opposed to regarding disability as a social phenomenon that brings certain people together into a disability community.

Indeed, disability studies readings of Shakespearian characters have a vexed critical history. In spite of the rapid growth of disability studies as a field of literary criticism, scholars applying disability theory to literary works have faced a wide variety of critical misconceptions. As David Houston Wood has noted, there is 'a general, if not institutional, reluctance to engage disability as a theoretical model for early modern topics', a 'scholarly hesitation to pursue early modern disability studies as a serious critical theoretical paradigm'.[2] Confronted with doubt about the definition of disability itself and haunted by accusations of anachronism, early modern disability studies has faced opposition from disability studies scholars as well as Shakespearians.[3] The question of what constitutes a 'disability' is notoriously difficult to define—thus, it is not surprising that to claim a Shakespearian character (any Shakespearian character) as disabled is often met with scepticism. Definitions of what counts as 'disability' in the modern world are often flexible and vague. For example, the Americans with Disabilities Act (ADA) offers a definition of disability that is extremely broad: the ADA claims that a person with a disability is a person who has 'a physical or mental impairment that substantially limits one or more major life activities; has a record of such an impairment; or is regarded as having such an impairment'.[4] According to this definition, the term 'disability' could apply to anyone with any kind of physical or mental difference that limits their activity in a significant way, anyone who has been medically labelled as 'disabled' or has a past history of the label, or anyone whom other people *perceive* to be disabled. This definition allows for an incredibly wide variety of conditions to be considered as 'disabilities', and it is only one possible definition among many.

A too narrow conception of what disability is easily misleads: when asked about disability and Shakespeare, many can think of only one character in Shakespeare's texts who might be considered as disabled—Richard III.[5] Although it is true that disability theory's engagement with Shakespeare initially focused primarily on Richard III (Mitchell and Snyder's famous reading in *Narrative Prosthesis* is a good example), more recent character-centred approaches have come to focus on a wide variety of characters and types of impairment: Caesar and Othello have seizures, *King Lear*'s Gloucester is blind, *The Taming of the Shrew*'s Katherine is described by Petruchio as walking with a limp, many of Shakespeare's tragic heroes are said to be 'mad' at one point or another, and disability readings in Shakespeare can be (and have been) extended to include obesity and infertility.[6] Early modern disability studies has also expanded to include non-Shakespearian Renaissance drama: *Early Modern Theatre and the Figure of Disability* and *Dissembling Disability in Early Modern England* are both recent books that offer character-based readings of disability in non-Shakespearian plays from the early modern era.[7]

Critical suspicion about these sorts of readings often stems from larger cultural anxieties about how disability should be defined. Uncertainty about defining disability sometimes betrays ableist fears that people who claim to have a disability may be 'faking it' in order to take advantage of offered accommodations or charity. In fact, people with 'invisible' disabilities frequently find that any claim to the label of disability in the absence of a visible marker of impairment is all too often met with suspicion and hostility.[8] Because my disability is not visible and I am able to pass as able-bodied, I once had a freshman class that adamantly argued with me, trying to convince me that I am not disabled. On other occasions, my need for accommodations during travel has been met with (inappropriate if not always unkind) interrogations about the nature of my disability. The status of 'disability' is an inherently ephemeral and flexible label. Impairments can be invisible, and pain almost always is. Some impairments can vary in severity from day to day. An impairment that is extremely difficult in one situation or environment may pose no difficultly in another. Thus, disability is always fluid, never static or fixed. In the face of this protean force, there is an overwhelming cultural desire to label, classify, and define different types of disabilities: indeed, disability studies scholars have argued that our modern cultural moment is obsessed with how disability is defined, labelled, and regulated.[9] It is these very concerns about accuracy and fraud that have produced a culture in which students must offer large amounts of paperwork and documentation (often large amounts of paperwork and documentation costing their families thousands of dollars) in order to secure even basic classroom accommodations. All of this harkens back to the medical model of disability—in a model in which the medical profession controls the definition of what disability is, the label of 'disability' requires the documentation of a physician or psychiatrist. Thus, the power to define disability is generally controlled by able-bodied medical authorities. This is yet another example of the ways in which people with disabilities can be rendered voiceless and in which their opinions about the experience of disability can be discounted or discredited. Our culture has taught people to regard disability with suspicion, and the reliance on official paperwork and documentation to assuage fears of malingering and fraud only serves to reinforce doubts in cases where copious medical documentation is lacking. If people with disabilities have to worry about accusations of fraud, it makes sense that readings of literary characters as disabled might also be met with suspicion from literary critics. If it is difficult to convince someone that an actual person is disabled, it will be even more difficult to convince him that an imaginary person is.

Even once the view of what constitutes disability is expanded to the widest possible scope and Falstaff's fatness is read as disability, thus proving the viability of disability studies readings in Shakespeare studies via the sheer number of characters considered, such character-centred readings must contend with ongoing claims that they are anachronistic. Modern disability terminology is complicated, and early modern disability terminology even more so. Leading scholars in disability studies, such as Lennard J. Davis, have argued that 'disability' as a concept is an invention of the late eighteenth and nineteenth centuries and that understandings of 'disability' arose in relation to the concept of the statistical 'norm'.[10] Consequently, some Shakespearians, such as Jeffrey R. Wilson, have argued that disability has no place in Shakespeare studies.[11] Because early modern people had no understanding of disability as an identity category, some scholars claim that early modern disability studies is fundamentally anachronistic. Thus, critics continue to contest the viability of 'crip' (a reclamation of the disability slur word 'crippled' as a marker of disability pride and identity) theory readings of early modern texts—even of characters, like Richard III, who openly describe themselves as having physical impairments. It is true that disability was not understood as a minority identity category in the early modern period, and although the term disability was first used to mean 'a physical or mental condition that limits a person's movements, senses, or activities' in 1492, 'deformed' was by far the more frequently used term in Shakespeare's day.[12] These objections to disability studies in Shakespeare are completely valid—and also absolutely irrelevant. Elizabeth Bearden points out that early modern people had a conception of what was considered 'natural' even if they did not use the concept of the 'norm,' arguing that 'Lennard Davis deftly excavates the development of the statistical norm and its implications for the social construction of disability, but he misses the mark in claiming that in premodern societies, no norming influence may be found'.[13] Certainly, it was possible for early modern people to apprehend differences in bodies and minds and to label those bodies and minds deemed different as 'deformed' or 'mad'.

More importantly, arguments against disability studies approaches to Shakespeare elide the potential of crip theory readings of the literary past to affect our understanding of the lived and embodied present. Shakespeare studies did not end in the early modern period. That is when it *began*. To eliminate the word 'disability' from discussions of Shakespeare is to ignore the modern uses to which Shakespeare is put. It is to ignore the modern readers, audience members, and actors who engage with Shakespeare and have disabilities. To say that the word 'disability' should not be used in relation to Shakespeare it to ignore modern oppression because of early modern semantics. Such arguments may seem to imply that, while the interaction of able-bodied people with Shakespeare's plays is a subject worthy of study, the engagement of people with disabilities with Shakespeare's plays is not a subject worthy of study. I will not argue that early modern people self-identified as disabled in the modern sense of the term. Rather, I will argue that since modern readers self-identity as disabled (or able-bodied), the way that those readers read Shakespeare matters.

Disability Access and Shakespeare

While there are limitations in and complications to applying disability theory to Shakespeare's characters, there are also key reasons to keep the fields of Shakespeare studies and disability studies in dialogue with each other. Character-based readings of disability contribute significantly to knowledge about what disability was in earlier cultures. There is value for modern people with disabilities in exploring the history of disability and its representation in earlier literatures and cultures: reclaiming the lost history of a cultural minority group is an undertaking well worth making.[14] More importantly, excluding disability as a subject of discussion from Shakespeare studies would be the ultimate symbolic failure of what disability studies terms 'access'. Disability access is achieved when a physical environment, information infrastructure, or social network is made available to someone with a particular impairment: the environment, infrastructure, or network is constructed in such a way so that someone with a specific impairment can easily and fully use it. Failures of access sometimes indicate failures of imagination—they may suggest that the designers of the environment or programme have failed to imagine that a certain kind of person exists. For example, a building that is constructed without ramps or elevators has failed to prepare for someone who uses a wheelchair: when the building was designed, the architect did not imagine that someone who could not walk would ever need to enter the building. When a theatre company puts on a three-hour production of *Hamlet* that would require me to sit still, in close proximity to the audience members on either side of me, in a large and noisy theatre containing hundreds of people, it did not occur to them that someone with my impairments might want to come to the show. In this way, failures of access are, at their best, unintentional failures of hospitality ('We are sorry—we did not imagine someone like you coming here'). At their worst, failures of access can be fundamental denials of equality that prevent someone with a disability from fully participating in society ('We feel that you are fundamentally unequal to an able-bodied person. How could someone like you possibly understand and appreciate Shakespeare?').

Failures of access mean that people with disabilities will not be able to participate (or fully participate) in a particular activity, will experience significant pain or stress in order to participate, or will need individual accommodations (changes to the environment or structure) in order to participate. Thus, creating access can have a substantial impact on people's lives. On the logistical level, creating access and/or providing accommodations makes it possible for more people to participate. On the ethical level, it allows people with disabilities to participate fully and equally in society. On the social level, it makes people with disabilities and their caregivers and family members feel welcome in spaces (whether intellectual, social, or physical) where they might not otherwise feel welcome. On the intellectual level, creating access and/or providing accommodations reminds all of us of the diversity and value of different kinds of human bodies and/or minds. For these reasons (and others), one of the major goals of the modern disability rights movement is to fight for equal access for people with disabilities. To exclude disability studies from Shakespeare studies would be a symbolic failure of access, a failure of the Shakespearian imagination to anticipate the presence of different kinds of bodies and minds.

If we are thinking specifically about equal access to education, art, and high culture, Shakespeare naturally becomes a contested zone for disability equality in the intellectual realm. That Shakespeare has a special cultural power, a symbolic import given to no other author in the Western canon, cannot be denied; thus, there are multiple reasons why questions of access to Shakespeare (rather than to the works of other authors) are particularly loaded. Social justice calls for the full equality and inclusion of people with disabilities—and that includes equal access to education. Whether we personally believe that Shakespeare is for everyone (I do not believe that Shakespeare is for everyone), it is clear that, at least in the English-speaking world, Shakespeare has become a symbol of elite culture and high art—knowledge of Shakespeare is often taken as the definitive proof of being well read and well educated. In many high schools, colleges, and universities, education includes Shakespeare, and his works are a standard staple of the curriculum. Thus, there are lots of students who have disabilities who are desiring to engage with (or are being required to engage with) Shakespeare. One of the primary arguments of this book is that an understanding of disability theory is essential for scholars, teachers, and directors of Shakespeare. Statistics suggest that as many as one out of four people could potentially be considered as disabled.[15] Since providing quality accommodations and pedagogical materials for users with disabilities requires a basic understanding of disability theory, teachers and directors of Shakespeare who wish to reach general audiences have a good reason to engage with disability studies. Surely Shakespeare should not be denied to one out of every four people. To return to the symbolic import of access as delineated above, to deny or refuse disability a place in Shakespeare studies is to deny that readers, students, audience members, scholars, and theatre practitioners with disabilities exist. As long as there are Shakespearians with disabilities in our classrooms, theatres, and libraries, we should have Shakespeare and disability studies—and not simply an engagement with literary character but also an engagement with the lived experience of users of Shakespeare with mental and physical disabilities.

If people with disabilities should have equal access to Shakespeare, there are still a lot of theoretical and practical questions that remain about how Shakespearians can or should work together to create disability access. Creating access is important, but it is not easy. One of the goals of disability studies as a critical field is to achieve universal design—to find a way to make everything accessible to everyone in all situations. As a theoretical ideal, universal design is wonderful. As a realistic achievement, it is impossible.[16] Some disability accommodations will naturally conflict with each other—for example, making music louder so that people who are hard of hearing can hear it will cause sensory overload for autistic audience members who are hypersensitive to sound.[17] In addition, a classroom attempting to provide universal design would be extremely expensive to create and time-consuming to maintain; and since one class would not be likely to contain students with every disability imaginable, it is probable that many expensive accommodations would regularly go unused. Although universal design is a theoretical ideal that can never be fully achieved, approaching pedagogy and theatrical practice with the mindset of universal design can have benefits for both students and audiences.

This book argues that there is a complex interdependence among theory, access, and inclusion—demonstrating the crucial role of disability theory in creating access and examining the ways that access may both open and foreclose inclusive dramatic practice. Those who want to create quality disability access need a basic understanding of disability theory: attempting to create access without an understanding of disability theory and the concerns of the disability rights movement can result in access that is superficial, unhelpful, or unsustainable. Sometimes it even results in 'access' that is not really access. For example, if a major premise of disability theory is that the embodied and lived experienced of disability is a valuable source of knowledge, and the motto of the disability rights movement is 'nothing about us without us', this would suggest that people with disabilities should have leadership roles in conversations about disability. Disability theory tells us that people from specific disability communities should be involved in planning and implementing programmes and performances that target people with the same kinds of impairments. Although this might seem like a common-sense suggestion, many programmes for people with disabilities are completely run by able-bodied people. When programmes for people with disabilities neglect central tenets of disability studies (such as failing to include people with disabilities in leadership and planning roles), the efforts of such programmes may unintentionally come across as patronizing. This is an example of access that is not really access—the programme might be designed for users or audience members with disabilities, but its leadership roles are only accessible for able-bodied people. If we wish to seek access, we can only seek that goal compassionately and responsibly by understanding and applying disability theory.

Over the past twenty years, Shakespeare theatres have been particularly innovative in the area of accessibility. This is, in part, because modern Shakespearians have always been driven by the need for access. Shakespeare has a central place in the curriculum, and making

Shakespeare accessible to students has long been a goal in the modern classroom. All (good) teachers try to make the subject matter accessible to their students. Shakespearians, in particular, are inspired to work hard in this area: four hundred years have already reduced the accessibility of the source text for lay readers and audiences. Indeed, popular culture often depicts Shakespeare as inherently difficult to understand. Shakespeare has become the classic symbol of that which is highbrow, and teachers and directors are charged with making his work accessible for everyone—from popular audiences to reluctant high schoolers. This means that Shakespearians are in a natural position to consider disability access; it makes sense that Shakespeare theatres would approach disability as just one more point of potential inaccessibility. After all, Shakespearians are already trained to think about access to Shakespeare's work in terms of social class, cultural relatability, and educational level. In fact, accessibility is so central to the Shakespearian mindset that 'access' is a key term in the mission statements of both the Royal Shakespeare Company and Shakespeare's Globe (for more on this, see Chapter 2). Unsurprisingly, these kinds of artistic visions have led Shakespeare theatres such as Shakespeare's Globe, the Royal Shakespeare Company, and the Oregon Shakespeare Festival to be particularly innovative in the area of disability access. Access can be artistic—it can be an integral part of the performance experience, shaping the interpretation both of the show and of Shakespeare's text.

Disability Inclusion and Shakespeare

One driving force in the search for accessible Shakespeare is the concept of 'inclusion'. Creating an 'inclusive' environment or programme means achieving access in such a way that people with a variety of diverse bodies and minds can participate equally. The theoretical questions that surround 'inclusive Shakespeare' become particularly complex in the case of programmes that employ Shakespeare's text as a form of therapy. The uneasy alignment of therapy with the concept of cure raises problems, since cure is a controversial topic in many disability communities. Some people with disabilities regard their impairment as an essential part of self-identity and do not want to be cured. Shakespeare therapy programmes are often in danger of replicating the power dynamics of the medical model, in which those who offer therapy and cure (the able-bodied teacher of Shakespeare) is placed in a position of power over the participants in the programme (people with disabilities). The search for genuine inclusion is fraught with complex ethical questions, in part because inclusion is difficult to define. In general, I would say that inclusion usually entails both participating equally and participating together. Some Shakespeare therapy programmes encourage both of those goals (equal participation for people with disabilities and able-bodied people, as well as people with disabilities and able-bodied people participating together). However, some Shakespeare therapy programmes encourage neither, offering unequal participation (therapy is given by the able-bodied and received by people with disabilities) and discouraging certain people from participating together (for example, offering separate performances that are designed for people with a specific type of disability rather than accommodating those audience members in performances intended for the general public). However, genuine inclusion does not always involve equal participation and participating together, both of which may sometimes be logistically impossible (see Chapter 3).

Some Shakespeare therapy programmes are based on beliefs that Shakespeare's plays somehow encapsulate what it means to be human. A popular culture belief that Shakespeare's plays express something uniquely human is common; however, the concept that Shakespeare's works contain something quintessential about the human may lead to the feeling that humans need Shakespeare—that Shakespeare is necessary *in order to be* human. [18] Such ideas may lead people to feel that to know and appreciate Shakespeare somehow proves that one is human.[19] If Shakespeare expresses the human and is needed to validate humanity, one may come to see Shakespeare as being able to restore humanity where it is believed to be lacking; from this line of thinking comes the belief that Shakespeare's language may be able to heal people with disabilities. Ableist attitudes have long imagined people with disabilities as less-than-people or not human.[20] Shakespeare therapy sometimes combines the search for treatment with a need to restore a human nature imagined to be missing, joining the medical model's agenda that seeks to eliminate disability from society through treatment or cure with the belief that those with disabilities will not be restored to full humanity without treatment or cure.

In addition, many Shakespeare therapy programmes are invested in the idea that Shakespeare is 'universal'. The belief that Shakespeare should belong to everyone may inspire a desire to create programmes that are inclusive. Thus, if there are disability communities that seem to lack access to Shakespeare, a colonial impulse is born: the able-bodied/neurotypical Shakespearian must find a way to bring Shakespeare to those who are perceived to be without him.[21] Ironically, Shakespeare therapy programmes present a situation in which inclusion may become exclusion: the impulse to cure is sometimes the impulse to eliminate disabled diversity. In this way, some Shakespeare therapy programmes may describe themselves as 'inclusive' (because they are making Shakespeare accessible to people with disabilities), when they, in fact, are not (since their motive to find treatment or cure ultimately seeks to end disability rather than to include it). When divorced from disability theory, the desire to include can be transformed into the drive to heal or cure and become, in both thought and practice, a form of covert exclusion. However, there are ways in which some Shakespeare therapy programmes function successfully without embracing the medical model and while fostering a genuine sense of inclusion for people with disabilities (see Chapter 3).

In the end, absolute inclusion may be impossible to achieve, but that does not mean that we should not strive for our classrooms, performances, and programmes to be as inclusive as possible. Maybe Shakespeare is not for everyone, but I would like for his works, performances of his works, scholarship about his works, and the body of knowledge and social networks that constitute Shakespeare studies to be available to the fullest extent possible to the largest and most diverse audiences possible. Of course, the very concept of making Shakespeare inclusive may raise issues for some teachers and scholars. First, academia places value on its status as that which is intellectually elite; to open academic spaces to different kinds of minds may raise questions, for some teachers, regarding academic rigour. For example, some might wonder whether Shakespeare's text should be made accessible to those with intellectual disabilities (people who test as having a low IQ). If so, there are plenty of questions about how full access to Shakespeare for those with intellectual disabilities might best be achieved. Second, many programmes and performances make Shakespeare accessible by making fundamental changes to Shakespeare's text. For example, Flute Theatre has experimented with productions in which Shakespeare's plays are pared down to be more accessible for audience members with mental disabilities.[22] If Shakespeare's text is simplified to be more accessible, some Shakespearians (seeing themselves as the guardians of intellectual rigour) might regard this not as the inclusivity of Shakespeare but rather as a reduction of Shakespeare. However, it is also possible to understand such use of Shakespeare as expanding Shakespeare—not only by including new audiences but also by encouraging specific disability communities to appropriate Shakespeare's texts in ways that are unique and authentic representations of those communities. I hope that this book will encourage scholars, teachers, and directors to create both artistry and intellectual rigour in ways that will engage the widest possible diversity of potential users of Shakespeare.

Cripping Shakespeare Studies

This book is organized to focus on three key themes that build on each other: theory, access, and inclusion. Understanding and employing disability theory (Chapter 1) are necessary to creating high-quality and meaningful access (Chapter 2). Without theory and access, there can be no real inclusion (Chapters 3 and 4). Each chapter focuses on a different kind of Shakespearian encounter with disability, from the theoretical and historical (Shakespeare studies' theoretical responses to the body of Richard III) to the practical and contemporary (accessible performances, Shakespeare-based therapy, performances including actors with disabilities). The first chapter, 'Cripping (and Re-Cripping) Richard: Was Richard III Disabled?', tackles key questions of terminology, identity, and historical identification. Offering a different kind of crip reading of Shakespeare's villainous king, this chapter follows the history of critical receptions of *Richard III* into the present, seeking to answer the symbolically central question of disability studies as a historical field: 'was Richard III disabled?'. Examining the ways in which the character has been interpreted by readers and portrayed in stage and film performance, the chapter addresses Shakespeare studies' historical resistance to Richard's disability. In doing so, the chapter calls into question the ideological frameworks of the interpretative traditions that have denied Richard's disability. Positing that this scholarly resistance parallels larger cultural tensions about uncertain definitions of what disability is and able-bodied resistance to the label of 'disability' in general, the chapter concludes that, according to the performance history and reception history of the play, Richard has always been, and will probably always continue to be, theoretically and politically crip.

After examining the theoretical complexities of early modern representations of disability in Chapter 1, the second chapter, 'Making it Accessible: Building Access in Shakespearian Spaces', turns to modern users of Shakespeare, examining the ways in which modern theatres have built access for audience members with disabilities. This chapter investigates practical responses to diverse access needs, with a particular focus on the impact that access may have on artistry. In order to do so, the chapter includes interviews with theatre practitioners (the Royal Shakespeare Company, Shakespeare's Globe, and the Oregon Shakespeare Festival) who have explored the possibilities of accessible Shakespeare. Combining an examination of theoretical concerns with practical experience, the chapter concludes with suggestions for best practices for accessible Shakespeare performances.

Chapter 3, 'Play for All: Shakespeare Therapy and the Concept of Inclusion', focuses on the idea of using Shakespeare's text as therapy. In particular, the chapter offers a case study of DE-CRUIT, a Shakespeare-based drama therapy for veterans with post-traumatic stress disorder, and the Hunter Heartbeat Method, a Shakespeare-based drama therapy for autistic children. The DE-CRUIT programme, while clear in its intent to work as therapy, functions outside of the medical model of disability in key ways: the programme is focused on fostering community support, as well as offering opportunities for veterans to appropriate Shakespeare's words in order to voice their own experiences of trauma and disability. The Hunter Heartbeat Method, however, stays more closely tied to the medical model: the programme uses rhetoric that may come across as potentially dehumanizing toward autistic people. Ultimately, the programme's colonial undercurrents are hinted at by its symbolic use of *The Tempest*, a play so often performed and read from a postcolonial perspective.

Chapter 4 explores a production of *A Midsummer Night's Dream* put on by a group of neurodiverse actors living in an assisted living facility, as well as the narrative that the neurotypical directors tell about the process of creating the production. Hank Rogerson and Jilann Spitzmiller's film *Still Dreaming* not only presents a traditional comedic conflict between the older and the younger generation but also explores the clash of cultures that may arise in encounters between the neurotypical and the neurodiverse. Although the documentary celebrates the comedic triumph of youth over age, it does not rely on tired tropes that prioritize neurotypical ways of thinking over neurodiverse ones. Rather, the film persuasively argues that those who are able-bodied and neurotypical can learn to understand disability culture, particularly neurodiverse ways of understanding relationships, accessibility, sensory perceptions, and time. Significantly, *Still Dreaming* presents Shakespeare, theatre, and the arts as the symbolic mediums through which such cultural exchange can take place.

The book's conclusion, 'The Brilliant Red of Shakespeare', discusses mental difference and unusual perceptions of artistry and art, questioning ideologies that present disabled difference as 'deficit'. The book ends by challenging Shakespearians to use disability theory to build access and to use access to create more inclusive theatres and classrooms.

1

Cripping (and Re-Cripping) Richard

Was Richard III Disabled?

One might suppose that the discovery and unearthing of Richard III's body, skeletal remains that obviously show evidence of physical impairment, would have eternally laid to rest (pun intended) arguments claiming that Richard III was not disabled.[1] It did not. The very idea that physical evidence of impairment might be *needed* to prove that Richard was disabled is, in my mind, every bit as bizarre as the original dispute itself. When the remains were unearthed in 2012, an argument about the status of Richard's physical body ('Was the historical King Richard III really disabled or did Shakespeare just depict him that way?') had been going on for hundreds of years. Like the never-ending debate about Hamlet's so-called 'madness', the fact that the argument exists and persists gives us important information about cultural norms regarding disability. First, it tells us that disability identity is a state of being that is always in doubt, a state of being that must be *seen*.[2] It tells us that disability is not believed unless seen—and sometimes not even believed when seen. Second, it tells us that disability signifies. (If disability wasn't assumed to signify, why waste time arguing about it in the first place?) Third, it tells us, according to all of the stereotypes, what kinds of characteristics disability is assumed to signify. (Richard was a villain, wasn't he?) Finally, it tells us that the cultural place of disability has not changed since the

Shakespeare and Disability Studies. Sonya Freeman Loftis, Oxford University Press (2021).
 DOI: 10.1093/oso/9780198864530.003.0002

Renaissance as much as we might like to think it has. Disability is still not believed unless seen, disability still signifies, and disability still signifies in certain stereotypical ways. These ways of thinking about disability both exist and persist in almost every discourse in which Richard III is discussed: from the historical society dedicated to the study of Richard's life to the media frenzy surrounding the discovery of his body; from popular media about English history to the scholarly discourse surrounding Shakespeare's play.

In all of these narratives about Richard III, the assertion of disability is met with doubt and opposition, and such opposition demands the answer of more 'evidence'—even in situations in which Richard III's physical impairment is already on display. Shakespeare is central to the literary canon, and disability studies seeks a place in that canon. Thus, 'was Richard III disabled?' has become the symbolic central question of disability studies as a historical field of literary criticism. In this chapter, I want to confront Shakespeare studies' historical resistance to Richard's (seemingly elusive, perpetually doubted) disability identity, examining the ideological underpinnings of the interpretative traditions that have so frequently denied Richard's disability. Just as the historical figure's disability was doubted and disputed until physical evidence was found, the very fact that the character has been described as having a disability by literary critics has been disputed and called anachronistic. The refusal to accept Richard as disabled, as both historical king and literary character, is a manifestation of a larger cultural denial that disability is ever really real in the first place. Ultimately, the denial that disability exists in Shakespeare is a denial that disability identity is a way to be human, that people with disabilities are a part of the supposed 'universal' human portrayed by Shakespeare. This impulse runs counter to stage tradition, which more often embraces the opposite, but equally troubling, stereotype in which disability is the sole defining factor in Richard's character. Thus, stage and film performances of Richard III often present a different sort of disability denial—a denial in which disability is presented as sensational and, thus, is imagined as relevant only when it can be presented as a fantasy that is interesting or exciting for the able-bodied audience. Unfortunately, such dehumanization in performance also implicitly separates disability from the so-called 'universal' human.

Resisting Richard's Disability in History

Perhaps the most disturbing stereotype perpetuated by discourse about Richard III is the sometimes subtle implication that he could not have been both a disabled person and a good person. Prior to the discovery of Richard III's remains in 2012, no physical evidence existed that the historical person, King Richard III, was a person with a disability. The primary evidence that associated Richard with disability was found in historical and fictional narratives written about him: the King's physical body was lost to time, his resting place unknown. Shakespeare's history plays clearly describe Richard as a character with physical impairments: Shakespeare's Richard has an arm that is 'like a withered shrub,' has a back shaped like a 'mountain,' has legs 'shape[d]' of 'an unequal size' and is 'disproportione[d] . . . Like to a chaos' (*3 Henry VI* 3.2.156–61). Some historical records about Richard, however, do not mention his physical impairments or atypical appearance. For many years the Richard III Society, a historical group in England, sought to redeem the reputation of the historical king, arguing that he was not the disabled villain that Shakespeare's plays depict him to be. Common cultural stereotypes associate disability with violence and villainy. Unsurprisingly, the group argued that the historical Richard was no villain and also that he was not disabled. The Richard III Society sought to 'promote, in every possible way, research into the life and times of Richard III, and to secure a reassessment of . . . the role of this monarch in English history'.[3] Reassessing Richard consisted primarily of trying to change public opinion regarding the two primary elements of his character that Shakespeare had popularized—his villainy and his disability. In defending the historical Richard from Shakespeare, however, the Richard III Society seemed unable to escape Shakespeare's influence, making the same mistake that Shakespeare makes—mistaking disability *for* villainy. Even as the Richard III Society attempted to defend Richard from Shakespeare's depiction, they reified the very stereotype that Shakespeare's depiction immortalised—the notion that Richard's disability *caused* his villainy: 'I that am . . . Deformed, unfinished, sent before my time / Into this breathing world scarce half made up . . . And therefore since I cannot prove a lover . . . I am determinèd to prove a villain' (*Richard III*

1.1.18–30). The Richard III Society was interested in defending Richard from a reputation for villainy: before evidence of his disability was found, they were also interested in defending him from a reputation for disability, as though disability and villainy are inextricably linked, as though the former would naturally lead to the latter.[4]

Thus, the Richard III Society's denial of Richard's villainy also became the denial of his disability. Prior to the discovery of Richard's body, the Society made statements such as, 'In reality, Richard was quite normal looking... [he] was known as an accomplished solider. He would not have been able to fight on horseback with heavy armour and weapons if he were Shakespeare's hunchback with a withered arm.'[5] The stereotypes implied by such claims are clear enough: the Society makes a false assumption here about what the historical Richard would or would not have been able to do because of his impairment. As Mitchell and Snyder put it, 'the Richard III Society's insistence that Richard disproves the slander of physical liabilities by the very fact of his accomplishments reinstates the belief that wherever accomplishment exists, disabled people do not.'[6] Judgements about whether Richard would have been capable of fighting in battle demonstrate the all-too-common assumption of able-bodied authority over the disabled body. As disability studies scholar David Bolt has observed, able-bodied people sometimes assert 'assumed authority' over people with disabilities and their bodies, making so-called 'common-sense' pronouncements about disability that incorrectly interpret what kinds of tasks it is possible for someone with a specific impairment to do.[7] The facts are these: the spine of Richard's skeleton shows scoliosis with an 80-degree curve, and the historical records of the time period state that Richard III fought in battle.

Yet contrary to this evidence, the popular imagination persists in doubt, questioning Richard's physical disability and his fighting ability, seeing the two as self-evidently contradictory. The excavation that discovered Richard's body was funded by the Richard III Society, and they were keenly disappointed to discover that Richard's skeleton showed signs of disability. When Richard's scoliosis was discovered, the Richard III Society organizer described it as a 'personal... disaster'.[8] When told that the archaeologists had not found a withered arm, the organizer responded by saying, 'The arms are ok?... Ah, some good news then'.[9] Hundreds of years of conjecture about

Richard's disability were based on the notion that Shakespeare used disability as slander—historians saw presenting Richard as disabled as a way for Shakespeare to undermine the York line and to make Henry Tudor the clear hero of the story. The lasting belief that the charge of disability would be an effective slander tells us, in itself, about the cultural place of disability in earlier times and in our own.

Indeed, prior to the discovery of Richard III's body, Shakespearians sometimes interpreted the historical records in ways that elided the historical king's disability. For example, prior to the discovery of Richard's body, Elizabeth Comber argued that he was not disabled: 'it is important to recognize that the historical Richard may very well not have been deformed, or at the very least was only mildly disfigured. He was, instead, made dramatically deformed by a burgeoning monarchy's need to discredit its predecessor.'[10] Note here the argument that either Richard had no disability or that his disability must have been 'mild'. Often, the desire to dismiss disability takes the form either of refusing to acknowledge impairment or of insisting that impairment should be understood as 'mild'—especially in cases in which people with disabilities are considered successful. Comber goes on to deny that Shakespeare's literary character experiences impairment because he triumphs in many endeavours:

> In addition to his success in winning love, throughout the play Richard satisfies his duties as Duke, serves as Lord Protector, becomes king and leads an army into battle. He is clearly able to satisfy the normal functions of a royal in spite of his hunchback... Perhaps this is why Richard is such as slippery character for disability studies to tackle. He forces the audience to question whether or not he even has a disability: A hunchback, the text tells us, yes: but a disability, the text tells us, no.[11]

Interpreting the achievements of Shakespeare's fictional character as evidence of a lack of impairment seems to imply that people with disabilities cannot be successful in their endeavours.

Comber goes on to read the historical narratives from the time period as indicating that the historical Richard III was not disabled: 'One such account is taken from the diaries of the Countess of Desmond, who after attending a royal pageant where she danced with Richard, remarked that "he was the handsomest man in the room except for his brother Edward, and was very well made".'[12]

The Countess of Desmond does not claim that Richard had no physical difference but, rather, describes him as 'handsome' and 'well made'—and a man with a disability may be both handsome and well made. Why didn't the Countess mention Richard's disability? Various reasons exist, but one potential answer is that the historical Richard III may have been able to pass as able-bodied in some situations, a subject largely unaddressed in the discourse about the historical figure.[13] People with disabilities passing as able-bodied is a common phenomenon in the modern era, and disability passing took place in earlier eras as well.

Given medieval stereotypes about disability as monstrosity, a medieval nobleman with a disability might have had some motivation to pass as able-bodied. Historian Ian Mortimer explains that early modern people may have equated disability with weakness: 'Richard III would undoubtedly have tried to hide the curve in his spine. The way a king looked was enormously important... When a king was ill, he would never reveal what was wrong with him. You could not have been seen to have that kind of weakness as a king' (Johnstone, *Richard III: The New Evidence*). In fact, when Henry VII displayed Richard's naked corpse in the streets as a sign of Tudor victory after the battle of Bosworth Field, it may have been the first time that some members of the public became aware of their monarch's physical impairment.[14] As one modern physician explains, the curve of Richard's spine caused by his scoliosis may not have been visible under his clothes: 'Although the scoliosis looks dramatic, it probably did not cause a major physical deformity. This is because he had a well-balanced curve... we identified no evidence that Richard would have walked with an overt limp, because the leg bones are symmetric and well formed.'[15] According to Jo Appleby, 'His trunk would have been short relative to the length of his limbs, and his right shoulder a little higher than the left. However, a good tailor and custom-made armour could have minimised the visual impact of this.'[16] Could Richard III have passed as able-bodied in some contexts? It seems likely that he could have. But what is most interesting to me is not the question of whether the historical Richard chose to pass as able-bodied, but the ways in which an able-bodied identity has been insisted upon and created for him by later generations of readers and scholars.

Resisting Richard's Disability in Theory

Even after the discovery of Richard III's body, some Shakespearian scholars have continued to deny his disability. Abandoning claims that the historical *person* did not have a disability, they now pursue claims that Shakespeare's *character* does not have a disability. In fact, some scholars claim that no Shakespearian character can have any kind of disability at all. This claim is both right and wrong—but the ways in which it is wrong are far more important than the ways in which it is right. First, a character is not a real person but a literary fiction. Because a 'character' exists as ink on paper, no character can have the attributes of living humans (no literary character really has a gender, race, sexual orientation, or disability in the sense that characters are fictive). Taken to its most extreme point, however, this line of argument would eliminate literary criticism as a field of study altogether (why are we studying works of fiction in the first place?). One reason we study works of fiction, I would argue, is because works of fiction reflect various aspects of our reality or the reality of the past. In short, it may be unreasonable to argue that a character who describes himself as 'deformed' is not disabled—at least in the fictive world that he inhabits.

Character-centred approaches to Shakespeare and disability studies have also, however, met with widespread critical suspicion and resistance due to claims of anachronism. As David Houston Wood has pointed out, there is 'a general, if not institutional, reluctance to engage disability as a theoretical model for early modern topics'.[17] Multiple scholars have argued that applying disability theory to Shakespeare is inappropriate, making their argument based on the terminology used in early modern times and, more importantly, on the differing ideologies reflected by such terminology. Lennard J. Davis, a leading scholar in disability studies, has argued that the concept of the 'normal' as we currently understand it originates in the late 1700s and 1800s, when the rise of modern medicine, concepts of the statistical norm, and industrialization led physicians (and employers) to increasingly define and measure the parameters of the 'normative' body (and the work or labour that body could be expected to produce).[18] Essentially, Davis argues that the creation of a concept of the 'normal' allows the identity category we currently understand as 'disability' to exist. Early modern people did not conceive of disability as we do now. In fact, although the term 'disability' existed in early modern times, it was rarely used to indicate a group of people with physical and/or mental impairments.[19] Outdated, and now offensive, terms associated with specific impairments, such as 'deformed' and 'lame', were much more common.[20] The very broad definition we have of disability as an umbrella category did not exist either, and many conditions that disability studies now include as 'disability' (addiction, obesity, chronic illness) were not necessarily thought of as belonging to the same category as early modern forms of disablement (blindness, 'madness', 'the lame').[21] More importantly, early modern people did not think of disability as a minority group with which a person might self-identify (that kind of concept is a much later invention that fits best with the era of the disability rights movement).

While anachronistic ways of approaching early modern disability certainly have their problems and limits, arguments against those kinds of readings can be taken to dangerous extremes. For example, Shakespeare scholar Jeffrey R. Wilson has argued in *Disability Studies Quarterly* against disability studies approaches to Shakespeare: although Wilson claims that his argument is not intended to 'invalidate the uses of disability theory in Shakespeare studies', he argues that, because of the anachronism of character-based readings, those wishing to address disability in Shakespeare studies should use the term 'stigma' rather than 'disability'.[22] Pointing out that 'there is no historical basis for the modern language of "disability" in Shakespeare's texts', Wilson goes on to argue that '*stigma* provides a better vocabulary for addressing the abnormal body in Shakespeare's works than *disability*'.[23] In the article, Wilson confesses that 'I worry that my reluctance to embrace disability as a useful vocabulary for Shakespeare studies will come across as . . . biased, discriminatory, and oppressive. Rather than shy away from this argument because of its ethical fraughtness, however, I want to take seriously the fact that terminological nervousness is a central feature of stigma.'[24] Acknowledging that people have strong feelings about terminology and minority embodiment (as well they should—the words we use matter) is not a defence of Wilson's choice of terminology; nor does it explain how his argument to exclude the term 'disability' from Shakespeare studies is not 'biased, discriminatory, and oppressive'. Wilson admits that we live in a world in which people are frequently 'deeply suspicious of someone's claim to be disabled', and notes that 'Our culture and history certainly exhibit highly undesirable traditions related to suspicion of the veracity of claims for disability.'[25] He fails to acknowledge, however, that Shakespearians who approach Richard III's disability with suspicion, denying that the character is disabled, are replicating this very dynamic in the pages of Shakespearian criticism. Indeed, one could argue that the inability of Shakespeare studies to accept Richard III as disabled is a function of what disability studies scholar Robert McRuer terms 'compulsory able-bodiedness'—our culture's summary demand that all bodies must be able bodies and the all-too-frequent refusal to acknowledge the presence of disabled others.[26] In day-to-day life, compulsory able-bodiedness often takes the form of assuming that someone with a disability is able-bodied and neurotypical because of the preconceived, and obviously incorrect, expectation that everyone one meets will be able-bodied and neurotypical. Thus, Wilson's denial of Richard III's disability replicates the cultural suspicion of disability that he claims to reject.

Just because the term 'disability' was not used in Shakespeare's time in the same way as it is used today does not automatically mean that it would be better for scholars to refer to early modern characters depicted as having physical or mental impairments by using the terms that were used in Shakespeare's time. Would it be better to describe Richard III as 'deformed'? It would certainly be more offensive to modern readers with scoliosis, and the same is true of using other outdated disability terms from Shakespeare's time such as 'crippled' or 'idiot'. Although it is important to acknowledge the differences in terminology and ideology between then and now, and to acknowledge that terminology affects and informs ideology, we should not *unnecessarily* offend modern readers. Unless there is a compelling reason to use outdated terminology, scholars should use the terminology now preferred by the minority group who may see their bodies and minds reflected in these characters—and currently, that term is 'disability'.

The resistance to disability studies approaches to Shakespeare is partly an argument about terminology and about what that terminology means—but it is also partly a misunderstanding of what disability theory is, who Shakespearians are, and what Shakespeare represents. Disability theory is a critical lens (like any other) that can be applied in diverse ways. Yet it is amazing how often disability studies scholars are asked (or expected) to defend the use of disability theory in relation to a character: how do we know that a particular character is disabled? Sometimes that question is relevant and important, but at other times it is not. Arguing that disability theory cannot be fruitfully applied unless a literary character can be 'proven' to have a disability greatly limits possible readings. More importantly, it may sometimes reify ableist discourses in which disability is perpetually treated as suspicious and must always be proven, forcing the literary scholar to take refuge in medical discourse to argue his or her point (must the critic delineate the 'medical symptoms' of the character?). Furthermore, character-based readings are only one way to apply disability theory in the field of Shakespeare studies: a major premise of this book is that a disability studies approach to Shakespeare employing character-based reading will inadvertently parallel the medical model of disability. The medical model sees disability as an individual 'problem' located in the bodies or minds of individual people: disability studies approaches to Shakespeare all too often regard disability as a singular phenomenon located in the body or mind of an individual character. The social model of disability, which reminds us that disability is a social construct, would encourage Shakespearians to look elsewhere—to examine the cultural spaces in which modern readers and audience members with disabilities encounter Shakespeare's plays. What about performances that include actors with disabilities? What about the use of Shakespeare's text in therapy programmes for people with disabilities? (For more on this, see Chapter 3.) What about students with disabilities who read and react to Shakespeare's text? There are many ways to apply disability theory to Shakespeare—including ways that function outside of literary character (and thus, outside of the medical model). In this way, limiting disability theory to individual literary characters may show a fundamental misunderstanding of what it means to do disability studies in the first place.

While crip theory may seem like an anachronistic approach to *Richard III*, it is, in fact, the most appropriate approach to an early modern work when modern responses have persistently denied and ignored the presence of disability in Shakespeare's play. 'Crip theory' is a subset of disability theory that reads literary works with a political and activist angle; growing out of and alongside queer theory, crip theory reclaims the disability slur word 'crippled' as a source of disability pride. As McRuer argues, that which is crip 'signif[ies] not simply an identitarian complement or alternative to dominant forms of embodiment but, rather, the will to undo compulsory able-bodiedness'.[27] In other words, crip theoretical approaches allow us to acknowledge and recognize disability in a larger culture that often elides and erases it. Such readings are in no way anachronistic—although the notion of the 'normal' as we currently understand it did not exist in Shakespeare's time, it certainly exists in ours. While Richard III did not live in an era of compulsory able-bodiedness, his story has been performed, read, and interpreted in times when compulsory able-bodiedness is common; and if crip theory is the way to counteract the impulse to ignore and deny disability in modern times, we need a crip Richard III.

In addition to misinterpreting disability theory as a critical approach, arguments against disability studies interpretations of Shakespeare may overlook who modern Shakespearians are and the broader scope of Shakespeare studies as a historical field. One of the major flaws in Wilson's argument is that it seems to assume that the interaction between Shakespeare and disability ended before the eighteenth century. It didn't. Shakespeare studies as a critical field began in the early modern period and continues into the present (and, I hope, into the future). To refuse to use the word 'disability' in discussions of Shakespeare is fundamentally to deny that Shakespeare's text has use and meaning in the present, to deny that modern people with disabilities (students, scholars, audience members) engage with Shakespeare's texts. In this way, arguments like Wilson's can become particularly dangerous: scholars must be careful that they do not become so caught up in textual debates about early modern terminology that they replicate modern oppressions in their scholarship. In addition, Wilson's argument seems to exclude performance studies as a part of Shakespeare studies. When audiences see an actor deliberately portraying Richard as a character with a disability (think, for example, of Antony Sher's famous performance of Richard as a character who uses crutches), the audience sees disability represented on stage. Both actor and audience bring their modern understanding of disability to such a performance. Thus, the argument that applying the term 'disability' in Shakespeare studies is too anachronistic ignores three key points: what disability studies is (a philosophy that encourages us to look beyond the medical model and, thus, beyond individual literary characters); who Shakespearians are (modern users of Shakespeare with physical and mental disabilities are a part of Shakespeare studies and their experiences are worthy of analysis and attention); and what Shakespeare studies is (a field that extends beyond the written words of the play text and into live performance).

Finally, such arguments—that readings of disability in Shakespeare studies are too anachronistic—fail to acknowledge what Shakespeare represents. In our current cultural moment, Shakespeare represents the literary canon, literature at large, high art, and education, both standing in as a symbol for these forms of knowledge and also forming (at least in the opinion of some people) an essential part of partaking of these forms of knowledge.[28] Shakespeare has been given credit for 'the invention of the human'.[29] His work is hailed as 'universal', and while many Shakespearians disagree with such bardolatrous extremes, the fact remains that these ideas are held by a surprising number of people and continue to be a part of discourse about Shakespeare (for further discussion, see Chapter 3). In some ways, I agree that there are no people with disabilities in *Richard III* (in much the same way that there are no women in *The Taming of the Shrew*). The role has been played, for many generations, by able-bodied actors who feign disability on stage.[30] Only fairly recently have we seen actors with disabilities being cast in the role of Richard III, bringing a more inclusive and authentic element to the depiction of disability in Shakespeare. Thus, *Richard III* is a play written by an able-bodied, as far as we know, author, with a villain who is, usually, played by an able-bodied actor, performed for a predominately able-bodied audience, and it presents an able-bodied fantasy in which disability, at least according to many interpretations, is what makes the villain so evil. On the other hand, to claim that disability has no place in Shakespeare is to claim, on some level, that if Shakespeare's text is credited with encapsulating the universal experience of 'the human', then people with disabilities are not a part of the human. Indeed, this is one of the major problems with claiming that Richard III is not disabled. A leader in the field of disability studies, Tobin Siebers, explains that '...disability studies takes Richard III as its standard-bearer...many critics in disability studies are eager to embrace a standard-bearer who suggests that power lies within the grasp of disabled people'.[31] Richard III is not the standard-bearer of disability studies because people with disabilities want to be represented as villains, as McRuer points out:

For most scholars in disability studies, perhaps only Charles Dickens's pitiful Tiny Tim is a more universally hated figure. Richard III is thus, from a certain critically disabled perspective, one of the two most despised characters in literature...this distaste for Richard in disability studies is not particularly difficult to comprehend, given the ways in which his 'monstrous' body logically explains his monstrous deeds. His 'deformity,' in other words, is generally causally connected to his evil machinations.[32]

Richard III is a standard-bearer for disability studies because he represents a place in Shakespeare for disability studies, because he reminds readers and audiences that people with disabilities are a part of the literary canon, a part of the so-called 'universal' Shakespeare, and a part of the human. Wilson's argument ignores the fact that real people with physical impairments lived in the Renaissance, ignores Richard's curved spine laid out and photographed on the table, ignores the objectification of Richard's body by the medical gaze of the present.

What is curious, however, about the standard-bearer of disability studies is that he won't stay 'cripped'. Here is what is truly fascinating about Richard III: we have ample evidence that the historical person on whom Shakespeare's character is based experienced impairment (what Lindsey Row-Heyveld calls 'the indisputable evidence of Richard's disability'),[33] and there is abundant textual evidence that Shakespeare's literary character has a physical difference that we would now describe as 'disability'; but even that kind of proof isn't enough for a Shakespeare scholar to claim Richard III as disabled. To apply crip theory to a character who calls himself 'deformed' and describes his limp, you'll have to write an essay explaining why you think the character has a disability in the first place. Such historical and critical denial of disability in the face of obvious disability reiterates and reinscribes into the pages of Shakespearian criticism cultural attitudes in which disability is stereotyped as uncertain, dubious, and inherently suspicious. The result is that we keep having to crip Richard and re-crip Richard and re-crip Richard.

Resisting Richard's Disability on Film

Indeed, public suspicion regarding Richard III's battle prowess has been so great as to serve as the primary inspiration for a recent documentary that interrogates the place of Richard's disability on the medieval battlefield. *Richard III: The New Evidence* interweaves interviews with physicians and archaeologists (who describe the state of Richard's skeletal remains and what it tells us about his physical impairments) with interviews with historians (who give context on medieval life and warfare).[34] Even more surprisingly, the documentary includes interviews with a young man named Dominic Smee, who has scoliosis and an 80-degree curve of the spine—in fact, the shape of Smee's spine is remarkably similar to the shape of Richard's. In the course of the documentary, Smee volunteers to act as a body double for the dead medieval king, subjecting himself to physical fitness tests, being fitted for battle armour, and learning horseback riding and sword fighting—all in an effort to prove that Richard III could have been a warrior.

From the beginning, the documentary is seeking evidence to confirm the truth of that-which has-already-been-confirmed. Viewers are shown the curved skeleton of Richard III at the beginning of the documentary and are told that the historical records indicate that Richard fought in battle. Indeed, historian Bob Woosnam-Savage explains in his interview that the historical records of the time, 'even those written by his enemies', present Richard III as one who 'fought well'. Richard was skilled not only in battle but also in horseback riding: 'Writing shortly after his death, the historian Polydore Vergil suggested that Richard was an expert horseman'. As Ian Mortimer explains, 'All successful medieval kings of England were warrior kings, there's no exception to that.' Enter Smee, who by acting as a body double will ostensibly allow the viewer to see Richard's disability in action on the battlefield. One might imagine that the evidence already presented (the spine displayed to show physical impairment and the historical narratives indicating that Richard was a warrior) would be enough for viewers to conclude that Richard III was a disabled warrior.

The remaining doubt is partially a factor of disability stereotypes (our culture falsely imagines people with disabilities to be unfit or weak) but also partially a failure of imagination. It can be difficult to imagine experiences of embodiment that are radically different from our own (this is a challenge for many people, both able-bodied and disabled alike). Indeed, people with disabilities often feel that others have a hard time gauging the true extent and severity of their impairments. As Tobin Siebers explains, 'Either disabled people are received as not as disabled as they are, or they are received as more disabled than they are.'[35] Many viewers, it seems, insist on overestimating the historical Richard III's impairment quite acutely, refusing to accept proof of a warrior with a disability, no matter what kind of evidence is given.

Another potential reason for this search for proof of the disability-that-is-already-evident is our cultural moment's intense focus on what disability studies scholar Ellen Samuels terms 'biocertification'. Biocertification is the need in the modern world to produce testimony, usually paperwork, to confirm disability identity: as Samuels explains it,

> Biocertification describes the many forms of government documents that purport to authenticate a person's social identity through biology, substituting written descriptions for other forms of bodily knowledge and authority. Biocertification materializes the modern belief that only science can reliably determine the truths of identity and generally claims to offer a simple, verifiable, and concrete solution to questions of identity. Yet in practice biocertification tends to produce not straightforward answers but . . . increased uncertainty . . . .[36]

Richard III lived in an era before biocertification—but this has not stopped modern audiences from feeling the need to categorize, label, and certify Richard's disability in the now. Although the skeletal evidence unearthed in 2012 is physical, visual, and scientifically verified, this proof of Richard's disability, *Richard III: The New Evidence* seems to claim, is also insufficient. As the documentary's narrator explains, 'the team will collaborate with Dominic [Smee] on a series of experiments to establish whether Richard could have worn a full suite of armour, led a cavalry charge, and fought in hand to hand combat'. The fundamental unwillingness to accept Richard as disabled may reflect ableist fears regarding disability fraud that inform misconceptions of disability. As Row-Heyveld has pointed out, in the early modern period, many people believed that 'disability is always inherently fraudulent'.[37] Such beliefs, of course, are not limited to the early modern period: Siebers notes 'the widespread suspicion that all disabled beggars are faking it' and points out that, 'When discovered by others, disabled people who pass are generally rewarded for their efforts with the accusation of deception.'[38] Indeed, disability frequently violates the stereotypes that seek to govern it: disability is sometimes not readily apparent or easy to see, and impairment can vary throughout a lifetime, or from day to day, or in the course of a single day.

Thus, *Richard III: The New Evidence*, while fascinating to watch, comes laden with a host of complex ideological problems from the documentary's outset. The notion that Richard's disability can be recreated by finding a body double with the same spinal curve as the medieval king is inherently flawed. The documentary's 'experiment', testing Smee's ability to engage in recreated medieval battles, relies on the stereotypical notion that all people with a particular disability label will be the same. Stereotypes that reduce people with disabilities to only a disability label are dehumanizing and forward many false assumptions. In reality, what one person with a particular impairment can do rarely predicts whether someone else with the same impairment will be able to do the same task. Factors such as physical fitness, past training, time to devote to training, pain tolerance, medications, community support, accessible environments, and individual personality, talents, and skills, among many other factors, influence if and how an individual will be able to complete a particular task. Although Smee defies modern stereotypes of 'health' and 'fitness' by learning to horseback-ride in a medieval-style saddle and wield a blade, his fabricated, reality-television-style experience is obviously different from the historical Richard's actual one. (To give just one example, as a medieval nobleman Richard would have likely had many years of experience with horseback riding and battle training.) Thus, the documentary's search for evidence of the disability-that-is-already-evident builds on common stereotypes about disability, implying that disability labels are static and simple and that people with the same impairment will be essentially interchangeable.

Early in the documentary, disability is depicted as simple deficit: the documentary begins by approaching scoliosis via the medical model of disability. Although what is said in the documentary about Smee's scoliosis is presented in the presumably objective tone of medical discourse, the presumed objectivity of the medical model of disability does not stop the documentary from objectifying Smee. Shirtless, Smee displays his back for the camera so that the curve of his spine can be compared to that of Richard's. The sterile display is potentially dehumanizing, comparing Smee's body to Richard's skeleton on the table; at least in these shots, the documentary encourages the viewer to focus on Smee's disability at the potential expense of his personhood. Throughout the documentary, the voice-over narrator (Christopher Eccleston) adopts the pose of an able-bodied voyeur who interrogates disability, asking questions such as 'what was the man with this body capable of?'. The narrator poses questions that presumably voice the doubts of the able-bodied and neurotypical audience in their regard of disability: 'The Leicester find and the scoliosis that bent his spine call Richard's fighting prowess into question. Could a man with such a twisted back really wear armour, ride a warhorse, and lead an army into battle?'

Overall, the documentary depicts both Smee's and Richard's disabilities as conditions that might cause failure or defeat. Although the medieval saddle provides some support, Smee's scoliosis still poses a potential disadvantage on the battlefield: the physical shape of his ribs restricts his lung capacity and, thus, affects his ability to take in oxygen during strenuous activity. The documentary interprets the results of Smee's physical fitness tests as 'show[ing] that Richard could have moved and fought well, but his stiff rib cage would have caused him to tire more quickly than other soldiers'. While stamina proves to be a challenge for Smee, the documentary finds (based on chemical analysis of Richard's bones) that Richard ate richly and drank too much wine in his years as king. Thus, the narrator concludes that 'The evidence suggests that it was ultimately the heavy burden of Kingship that defeated Richard not his scoliosis'. The historical records have never suggested that Richard was defeated by his own disability but, rather, by Henry Tudor and his army; but given modern disability stereotypes, it is not surprising to see the documentary depict disability as a challenge that might cause defeat.

In the end, the documentary depicts Richard and Smee as heroic men who overcome the adversity of disability through hard work and bravery; in this way, the documentary's narrative takes on the form of the 'heroic overcomer' story. The 'heroic overcomer' is a stereotypical figure in narratives about disability, one who finds a metaphorical cure by 'conquering' disability in some way. The problems with these kinds of overcoming narratives are manifold. By depicting disability as a challenge to be overcome and praising those who overcome, such stories seem to cast aspersions on people with disabilities who cannot or do not overcome. By casting overcoming as virtue, such stories often hold up cure, normalization, and passing as unquestionably desirable outcomes. By depicting people with disabilities as 'inspirational', such stories may abuse conceptions of disability as an inherent negative and objectify people with disabilities in order to make able-bodied people feel better about themselves and their own challenges through comparison. Smee is triumphant in the documentary's ending, as he realizes that other people and their preconceived notions, not his impairment, were holding him back:

> It makes me feel a lot better about myself, knowing that I can do something that ordinary healthy people struggle with—and yet I've managed to do it despite having this condition...It's made me realise that my back wasn't holding me back as much as I thought it was. I thought that it was—'I can't do these things because of my back. It is getting in the way... and I shouldn't do this, and I shouldn't do that' and listening to all these people say, 'no, no, no, don't do that you'll be at risk of this.' And really it was my own level of fitness that was holding me back, and it is completely possible to do these things. (Johnstone, *Richard III: The New Evidence*)

Smee's pride in his hard work, new skills, and gained insight bleeds over into the documentary's narrative about Richard III. As the documentary conflates the two disabled figures (one modern and one early modern), Richard, too, is presented as a heroic overcomer, as a figure who somehow conquers disability through determination and hard work. Indeed, Mortimer, during his interview in the documentary, describes Richard III as 'a man who was struggling against adversity and could be a bit of a hero'. In a fade-out, the image of a flag with St. George's red cross bent over on itself, folded by the wind, immediately follows an illustration of Richard's curved back, presenting the image of the folded cross as parallel to the curve of his spine. The overlap of the images suggests a potential patriotism underlying that which is cripped, as well as the potential heroism of an English king who 'triumphs' over disability.

Yet the heroic overcomer, like Richard III himself, is a disabled figure who fundamentally will not stay cripped. Such stereotypical figures all too often suggest that disability can be erased through hard work or accomplishment; through the virtue of determination such figures are seen as being able to symbolically un-crip themselves. Ultimately, Richard III was 'not disabled', the documentary concludes, because he was able to fight in battle. As the narrator explains, 'Dominic [Smee] has laid to rest the myth that Richard was a weak and feeble man. Instead, we have discovered that he was dissolute *but not disabled*, a hard drinker and a big eater but a skilled fighter. He could have led a heavy cavalry charge and fought in brutal hand-to-hand combat. He emerges as Britain's last true warrior king' (emphasis mine). Ironically, the documentary concludes its validation of Richard as a disabled warrior by erasing the effect of this discovery, looping back on itself, and asserting that Richard was not disabled. After making the villainous Richard into a disabled hero, the documentary ends by asserting that there can be no disabled heroes after all.

Revealing and Concealing Richard: Displaying Disability in *The Hollow Crown*

While historical and critical traditions have long denied Richard's disability, performance traditions, grounded in the physicality of the actor's body, have been unable to do so. Although historians and scholars have insisted that Richard was not disabled, implicitly erasing Richard's disability from public discourse, there is a long stage tradition of sensationalizing the sight of Richard's disability. Such sensationalized performances, in which able-bodied actors feign disability, play on the long history of disability as freak show. Ironically, this sensationalizing of disability, the stereotypical rendering of disability as that which is hypervisible, is also a form of erasure. By simplifying disability and exploiting it for entertainment value, such performances often reduce and simplify Richard's character by presenting his disability as the *only* attribute of his character worthy of attention and focus. Thus, both the erasure of disability and the sensationalizing of disability hold the same stereotype at their roots—the notion that disability must be seen and displayed. Indeed, *Richard III*'s long history of exploiting fictional disability as visual display manifests itself most recently in the BBC's *The Hollow Crown: The Wars of the Roses* (2016).[39] Throughout the series, the show playfully engages disability as visual display. Alternately withholding and then revealing Richard's disability at key moments, *The Hollow Crown* builds on the stage and film traditions that came before it, often casting the sight of physical difference as scintillating or sensational in a self-aware and campy way. The show's constant visual focus on Richard's body (and therefore disability) functions on multiple levels, as the show winks at Benedict Cumberbatch's reputation and popular following as an able-bodied actor known for his good looks, while simultaneously revealing and concealing Richard's body in ways that draw attention to themes of reflection and self-reflection already present in Shakespeare's text. In doing so, *The Hollow Crown* manipulates cultural norms dictating that disability is that-which-must-be-seen in part by creating suspense in those moments in which it is not seen. By toying with the long stage history of displaying and exploiting Richard III's disability for the benefit of the able-bodied audience, the show brings a cagey self-awareness to its directorial choices regarding disability as display. By sensationalizing Richard, the series dehumanizes the disabled villain in a way that draws attention to this very act of dehumanization.

First, the show dramatically conceals and then reveals Richard's body in ways that work to create suspense for an audience familiar with English history. This tactic works, in part, because of the long history of displaying and exploiting Richard's disability on stage. The young Richard first appears at the end of *Henry VI, Part I*. Richard's father, York, walks through his house calling for his sons. Three of his children appear readily, and as they are discovered by the camera, their father calls each by name, 'Edward, George, Edmund'. The pause after this incomplete list leaves the audience time to wonder: where is the most infamous of the sons of York? As his father shouts, 'And Richard?', the camera focuses on a darkened archway leading to an exterior door. Unlike his three brothers, who stand plainly visible in the bright light of the house, the boy who enters through the darkened door is obscured in shadow. His limping gait is immediately noticeable, although his face and body remain hidden from the viewer. As he moves slowly toward the camera, the episode ends without revealing the details of the shadowy figure. Thus, the first thing viewers of *The Hollow Crown* see, in looking for and at Richard, is his disability. Yet the actual sight of Richard's body remains cloaked in mysterious shadow—viewers see only the outline of a small, dark figure limping toward the camera. This revealing yet concealing of Richard's body ends the first episode on a suspenseful note. The obscured figure moving toward the camera promises that Richard III is coming but not yet arrived in the storyline. Cumberbatch's star power means that viewers tuning in specifically to see him will have to wait until the second episode (*Henry VI, Part II)*, and the potential visual spectacle that Richard's famous disability affords the implied able-bodied viewer is also temporarily withheld from the audience.

Henry VI, Part II, continues this motif of simultaneously revealing and yet concealing Richard's body, strategically withholding the sight of disability. Richard wears long sleeves and gloves that hide his immobile arm; capes that pin on one side (always the left) frequently cover both his left arm and the shape of Richard's back. While Cumberbatch plays the part with an overt limp, leaning heavily to one side, such costuming choices suggest a character who makes some effort to downplay his physical difference. The actor draws attention to Richard's disability in other, more subtle, ways: for example, he clearly implies that Richard's impairment causes him pain, uttering a barely audible groan each time that Richard must kneel. While elements of Cumberbatch's performance obviously indicate Richard's physical impairments, capes and battle armour cleverly conceal the implied differences in the character's imagined body. *Henry VI, Part II,* like *Henry VI, Part I,* ends with a scene in which Richard's character serves as a teaser for the audience, enticing them to view the next episode. As the happy inhabitants of the throne room cry 'Long live Prince Edward', the camera focuses in on Richard, who cradles the baby Prince in his mobile arm and looks at the infant with clearly sinister intent. Right before the blackout, the villainous Richard begins to smile. While *Henry VI, Part I,* teases the audience with the promise of displaying Richard's disability (a display that does not appear in *Henry VI, Part II), Henry VI, Part II,* ends by tantalizing the audience with the promise of displaying Richard's violence. Given cultural stereotypes about disability and violence, it is significant that the two episodes' parallel endings use each as an enticing promise of scandalous or forbidden display for the viewer. At the same time that disability and violence are offered (and in some ways, conflated), the further display of Cumberbatch's fictionally 'disabled' body, so teasingly withheld in the first two episodes, is also promised: viewers will have to wait to see how the body of the able-bodied actor will be transformed by fictional disability. In offering both the display of disability and the display of further violence at the ending of each episode, the series deliberately promises, and then withholds, aspects of Richard's character that are considered taboo and sensational.

The opening of the third episode revels in the long-withheld display of Richard's disability. *Richard III* opens with a shot of a chessboard, and then a shot of Richard's hand suspended over it: a golden ring emblazoned with a large 'R' tells viewers that Richard is the player even before they see him. The camera pulls back gradually, unveiling Richard's body bit by bit, enjoying the slow reveal of that which has been so suspensefully concealed over the past two episodes. After the black knight takes the white knight, Richard begins his opening soliloquy. Nude to the waist, the villain is bent over a chessboard in which he plays a game of strategy with himself. It takes *The Hollow Crown: The Wars of the Roses* four hours to reach this dramatic revelation of Richard's body. As Richard leans over the chessboard, the curve of his back made even more prominent by the fact that he is bent double over the table, the camera moves behind him, rotating around Richard in a circle. The soundtrack makes a soft wailing sound in the background as the camera lingers on Richard's curved spine, a sound clearly evocative of pain. This 360-degree view of Richard showcases the curve of his back and, without his long sleeves and gloves, his left arm is finally fully visible. The camera's circular movement, which allows the viewer to see Richard's body from all angles, emphasizes the drama of the long-withheld view of Richard's seminude body, visually mirroring the way in which Shakespeare's opening soliloquy draws attention to Richard's impairment. Significantly, this version of *Richard III* begins with the display of Richard's curved back: viewers see Richard's disability fully exposed before they even hear him speak his first line. Thus, viewers who have skipped *Henry VI* will see Richard's back before they see his face.

Of course, the image of Richard's atypical back is here ghosted by the audience's previous knowledge of Cumberbatch—an able-bodied actor particularly famed for audience focus on his body as a source of desire. Thus, Cumberbatch's famous and 'normative' body is held in the audience's mind in contrast to Richard's body: the camera with its 360-degree spin emphasizes the difference between the character's fictional body and the body of the able-bodied actor. *The Hollow Crown* thus toys with the popular culture image of Cumberbatch by contrasting that which is considered 'normative' or idealized with a character who believes he 'cannot prove a lover' because his embodiment is regarded as different from that of his peers (*Richard III* 1.1.28). This moment of blatant display invites the audience to stare at Richard's disability, as *Richard III's* opening soliloquy always does—but the dynamic of that staring is further emphasized through the denial of the able-bodied gaze for four hours, the casting choice of an able-bodied star, the decision to present the soliloquy half-nude, and the camera's circular movement around Richard's body. Through such choices, the series cleverly manipulates the sight of disability, carefully choosing when and how Richard's disability is displayed. In doing so, *The Hollow Crown* manipulates common stereotypes about disability as a visual phenomenon, juxtaposing scenes in which Richard's body is hidden with scenes in which it is deliberately laid bare to the gaze of the able-bodied audience.

Even more significantly, *The Hollow Crown* uses the repeated motif of reflection to further emphasize Richard's focus on his own physical appearance. Images of mirrors and reflection in the Shakespearian source text suggest that Richard has a near obsession with his physical appearance: Richard's focus on his looks causes him to conclude in this opening soliloquy that he is not 'made to court an amorous looking-glass', and he claims that he will 'be at charges for a looking-glass' after his courtship of Anne (*Richard III* 1.1.15; 1.2.242). In his opening soliloquy, he also talks about seeing his 'shadow in the sun'—another kind of reflection that may show the shape of his body and, thus, reveal the outline of his disability in his silhouette (*Richard III* 1.1.26).

Indeed, Richard's mother describes him as 'one false glass' in which the image of her late husband is falsely reflected:

> I have bewept a worthy husband's death,
> And lived with looking on his images.
> But now two mirrors of his princely semblance
> Are cracked in pieces by malignant death
> And I for comfort have but one false glass,
> That grieves me when I see my shame in him.
>
> (*Richard III* 2.2.49–54)

Because of his disability, Richard's body (unlike the bodies of his brothers) deviates from the image of his able-bodied father, offering a false reflection. His bodily difference is here depicted as both inherently 'false' and deviant as well as that which brings 'shame' on his family. *The Hollow Crown* picks up on this imagery and makes it central to the depiction of Richard's character. Richard's obsession with his reflection begins in the second episode: as he delivers the line, 'Why, I can smile, and murder whiles I smile', Richard holds his sword up so that he can see his reflection in it. As the camera focuses in on Richard's smile reflected in his sword, it presents a perfect image of his deceptive charm as weapon. But while Richard is pleased to see his image reflected in a murder weapon as he is on his way to kill Henry VI, he often turns away from his image when it is shown to him by others.

Indeed, Richard inevitably seems to be angered by the sight of himself when his image appears in the third episode. Richard gazes at his reflection in a golden goblet as he confesses that he was not made 'to court an amorous looking-glass'; his anger in this scene is clear, as he slams his mobile hand against the table, rattling the chessboard. Later, this image of reflection returns in Margaret's climactic cursing scene: Margaret holds up a handheld mirror in order for the characters to see themselves as she shrieks curses. Richard, of all the characters, turns his face away most fiercely from Margaret's mirror. He sees himself as 'deformed' and 'unfinished', so he flinches away from his reflected image. Meanwhile, flashes of the future Margaret predicts appear in the mirror, such as a vision of the princes smothered in the tower. In this scene, Richard's unwillingness to face his own image because of physical difference becomes a symbol of his metaphorical inability to face his crimes. The images in the mirror, the image of disability, and the image of violence are all images Richard turns away from and denies—he cannot stand to see his true self when Margaret shows it to him. Thus, his turning away from the mirror is a fundamental denial of both his physical form and his violent nature. Richard is haunted by Margaret's mirror—by his own reflection as shown to him by her curses. For example, after his coronation Richard looks at himself wearing the crown in the reflection of a dagger but drops the weapon abruptly when Margaret appears in the reflection, apparently standing behind him.

This motif of Richard's inability to face his own image reappears prior to the battle of Bosworth Field. His dream sequence begins with Margaret walking into his tent and holding up the mirror, in which the image of Henry VI appears. Margaret guides Richard through a palace full of ghosts, and the dream sequence ends with her again holding up the empty mirror, which now fails to reflect Richard's image but, rather, shows only darkness. While the dream sequence in Shakespeare's text confronts Richard with images of the violence he has done, the dream sequence in *The Hollow Crown* conflates Richard's violent nature with his disability, as Richard is horrified by a mirror that reflects both the crimes he has committed as well as serving as a symbol of his bodily difference. Finally, as he grapples on the ground with Richmond in the battle's finale, Richard sees Margaret standing above him with the mirror in the moment of his death. In the end, *The Hollow Crown* suggests, Richard is unable to escape from the image of Margaret's mirror, which magically conflates his villainous actions with his disabled physicality. Blood and mud mingle as Richard lies on the ground in the centre of a circle of onlooking soldiers, his disabled body a spectacle even in death.

In short, *The Hollow Crown*, instead of undermining or avoiding disability stereotypes, leans into them with a campy and self-aware directness. Rather than downplaying or denying the early modern source text's offensive assumption that disability is spectacle, the series amplifies those aspects of Shakespeare's history plays. The show creates suspense by promising and then strategically withholding the sight of Richard's disability, cleverly manipulating cultural stereotypes dictating that disability must be seen. The series takes a kind of perverse delight in reminding the audience of disability stereotypes as it initially denies the view of disability, only to later revel in and exploit it. *The Hollow Crown* also further conflates disability and villainy in its repeated motif of mirrors and reflections, implying that Richard cannot face himself both because of his disability and because of his villainy. Indeed, the show's cagey embrace of Shakespeare's stereotypical depiction of a disabled villain may suggest that a campy and self-aware directness has become the only way to successfully present *Richard III*, with all of its tired disability stereotypes, in the modern era. Ultimately, *The Hollow Crown* makes no effort to deny that Richard III was disabled; rather, it manipulates and builds on long-standing ableist stage traditions in which Richard III's disability is *the* defining feature of his character.

Internalizing Oppression, Cripping Richard

While *Richard III: The New Evidence* depicts its main characters (Richard/Smee) as potentially heroic, it is not just the (presumed able-bodied) narrator who makes such judgements: Smee himself feels that he gains new self-confidence by impersonating Richard III. As Smee concludes, performing as Richard 'makes me feel a lot better about myself' (Johnstone, *Richard III: The New Evidence*). Smee's reclaiming of Richard as a disabled hero not only suggests the power and significance that a modern reader or audience member with a disability might find in Richard but also simultaneously hints at the internalized oppression that many people with disabilities experience. In the beginning, before finding potential heroism in Richard, Smee needs to 'feel a lot better' about himself and his disability in the first place. By the ending of the documentary, Smee realizes that he has been listening to social norms that have told him his disability makes him incapable: listening to other people's perception of his disability, Smee realizes, has been a part of what was 'holding [him] back' from physical activity. Internalized oppression, a state in which people adopt the stigmas levelled against them and replicate those stigmas in their own attitudes and thoughts, is a common experience for people with different kinds of disabilities.

Although Richard's disability has been a popular topic for literary analysis, scholars have not approached Richard's character through the lens of this kind of internalized disability oppression—perhaps in part because Richard's status as a character with a disability has so often been called into question in scholarly discourses. Over the years, many possible readings have been done of Richard III's disability in Shakespeare's play. One of the most popular and long-lived is the tradition that Richard's disability causes his villainy—his physical difference becomes his motivation.[40] This is the vilification of impairment—not just the medical model's notion that disability always represents loss, but the additional idea that one would naturally seek redress for that loss through nefarious action.[41] Other critics and actors have concluded that Richard hates able-bodied people because of the ableist stigma that is levelled against him, and he reacts with violence.[42] More recently, scholars have suggested that Richard is intensely aware of his own disability and performs disability to manipulative effect, playing off the other characters' preconceived notions about disability.[43] It is possible, however, to imagine a *Richard III* in which neither disability nor disability discrimination cause villainy. Indeed, Richard's own attitude toward disability does him more harm than the attitudes of the people around him. Like able-bodied and neurotypical people, people with disabilities have agency, and they make choices. It seems clear that Richard chooses to do violence and not that disability or social discrimination cause violence. In fact, Richard's character shows signs of internalized disability oppression—he believes so firmly that his disability indicates a villainous destiny that he comes to accept labels such as 'villain', 'false', and 'treacherous' (*Richard III* 1.1.30; 1.1.37).

Shakespeare's Richard III is a character who believes that impairment defines his life. Richard's body does not match the bodies around him—and he knows it. It is not just a fact that he is keenly aware of but also one that profoundly defines his character. As Siebers explains, 'The distinguishing feature of Richard is his self-consciousness of his own status as "disabled".'[44] (Note Siebers's use of scare quotes around 'disabled', clearly indicative of the widespread opposition disability studies scholars have encountered in their attempts to claim Richard as crip.) If his opening soliloquy is any indication, the character spends quite a lot of time thinking about his non-normative body: indeed, it is the primary subject of his famous first speech. Impairment is not just a significant fact audiences know about Richard, it is often the first fact they know about him—perhaps because Richard sees his physical difference as central to his understanding of himself. (Of course, how and when Richard's disability is introduced is partially a factor of whether audiences have seen the *Henry VI* plays prior to watching *Richard III.*) Although I will be accused of anachronism if I argue that Richard identifies with his crip nature, it would be to fundamentally contradict the text of the play to argue that Richard's physical difference has nothing to do with his sense of self. In his opening soliloquy, Richard overtly references his physical difference eleven times. These repeated references to his impairment allow him to describe disability as both physical reality and social construct: he describes himself as 'halt[ing]' (walking with a limp) but also claims that he 'cannot prove a lover' (seeing himself as less desirable and as lacking in social confidence, at least romantically) (*Richard III* 1.1.23; 1.1.28). He describes himself as someone who is discriminated against by others, and his belief that all possible partners would reject his romantic overtures suggests social discrimination. Whether his impairment actually defines Richard's life or not is irrelevant—what matters is not whether impairment defines his life but whether Richard believes that it does. His disability does not make him evil. Other people oppressing him do not make him evil. His own internalization of disability oppression and hate places him in a space in which he comes to believe that he is evil—and he chooses to act accordingly.

Thus, the opening soliloquy of *Richard III* could be seen as neither a false statement about how disability leads to villainy nor an equally false indication of how social discrimination naturally results in retributive violence but, rather, as a speech that is simply about self-hate. With the frequent repetition of 'I', the speech is self-directed and full of anger and self-loathing. Like many soliloquies in Shakespeare, Richard's opening speech is more about what is felt on the inside than what is displayed on the outside: thus, it is interesting to note how many interpretative traditions have historically understood this soliloquy *via* Richard's outside. His physical disability is a visual distraction. As Genevieve Love explains, 'Richard begins the play by calling attention to a theatrical body that he displays to the audience, a body laden with expectations, but he does not tell the audience exactly what they see.'[45] Row-Heyveld notes that 'He appears alone on stage, the only one of Shakespeare's characters to begin a play in soliloquy, and his solitariness, coupled with a speech about the limitations of his body, invites playgoers to look at him.'[46]

It is important to note, however, that Richard is primarily telling the reader not about his disability, nor about how other people treat him because of his disability, but about how he has come to feel about his disability:

> Now is the winter of our discontent
> Made glorious summer by this son of York;
> And all the clouds that loured upon our house
> In the deep bosom of the ocean buried.
> Now are our brows bound with victorious wreaths,
> Our bruisèd arms hung up for monuments,
> Our stern alarums changed to merry meetings,
> Our dreadful marches to delightful measures.
> Grim-visaged war hath smoothed his wrinkled front,
> And now—instead of mounting barbèd steeds
> To fright the souls of fearful adversaries—
> He capers nimbly in a lady's chamber
> To the lascivious pleasing of a lute.
> But I, that am not shaped for sportive tricks
> Nor made to court an amorous looking-glass,
> I that am rudely stamped and want love's majesty
> To strut before a wanton ambling nymph,
> I that am curtailed of this fair proportion,
> Cheated of feature by dissembling nature,
> Deformed, unfinished, sent before my time
> Into this breathing world scarce half made up—
> And that so lamely and unfashionable
> That dogs bark at me as I halt by them—
> Why, I in this weak piping time of peace
> Have no delight to pass away the time,
> Unless to spy my shadow in the sun
> And descant on mine own deformity.
> And therefore since I cannot prove a lover
> To entertain these fair well-spoken days,
> I am determinèd to prove a villain
> And hate the idle pleasures of these days.
>
> (*Richard III* 1.1.1–31)

The second half of Richard's opening soliloquy has eight repetitions of the word 'I', which are held in contrast to its first half's six repetitions of the word 'our'. Richard feels different, alone, and alienated—he does not see his 'I' as fitting in with the communal able-bodied 'our'.[47] As McRuer argues, 'Because of his disability, Richard is a misfit in a time that apparently delights in beautiful and fashionable images. Richard thus hates the future portended by the son of York on the throne and villainously chooses to eschew the vacuous sunny disposition . . . that the times demand.'[48] I would like to push McRuer's reading even further by noting that what is significant in this speech is not that Richard is an outsider because of his disability but, rather, that Richard *believes* he is an outsider because of his disability. Here, at the very beginning of the play, he only manages to speak four lines before referencing the human body: 'Now are our brows bound with victorious wreaths, / Our bruisèd arms hung up for monuments' (*Richard III* 1.1.5–6). He speaks of human 'brows' but also of 'arms', and while the 'bruisèd arms' referenced are ostensibly war weapons that are no longer in use ('hung up for monuments'), it seems quite likely that Richard, who Shakespeare describes elsewhere in the play as having a 'withered' arm, makes a pun that obliquely references his physical impairment (*Richard III* 3.4.69).

However, records about the historical Richard's prowess in battle may raise other questions about the Shakespearian character's famous discontent. Richard is discontented because battle has ended, while everyone else is happy about it. It is possible that the 'bruisèd arms' which he must now abandon were prosthetics for his 'withered' arm. If he excelled in war, perhaps that is why he misses it now and seeks successfully to bring it back again. If it is easier for Richard to pass in armour and to move on horseback, 'mounting barbèd steeds', rather than to dance, 'caper[ing] nimbly', is it really surprising that he laments the ending of war (*Richard III* 1.1.10–12)? Although Shakespeare's Richard feels that he is 'not shaped for sportive tricks' and thinks that he will not fare well in the courtly world of love, the historical stories which Shakespeare may have inherited suggested that Richard found himself well shaped for war (*Richard III* 1.1.14). Yet in associating himself with battle, Richard also associates himself with that which is often viewed as violent and evil: he links himself in rapid succession with 'winter', 'clouds', 'bruisèd arms', 'stern alarums', 'dreadful marches', and the 'wrinkled front' of 'Grim-visaged war' (*Richard III* 1.1.1–9). Richard associates himself with battle, an image that does not match modern stereotypes about disability, but one that does match the historical record regarding the life of King Richard III.

While scholars have frequently read the opening soliloquy as indicating that Richard's body becomes his destiny, that he is doomed to villainy by his body or by the society that discriminates against that body, this opening speech emphasizes how Richard thinks and feels about his own body—not how other people see it. It is Richard's interpretation that he is separated from and in symbolic juxtaposition to the communal 'our' that is glad of peace. It is Richard's belief that he is 'not shaped for sportive tricks / Nor made to court an amorous looking-glass' (*Richard III* 1.1.14–15). It is Richard's understanding that he is 'curtailed of this fair proportion, / Cheated of feature by dissembling nature, / Deformed, unfinished, sent before my time / Into this breathing world scarce half made up' (*Richard III* 1.1.18–21). Although the unusual circumstances of his birth may be factual, his interpretation of it—the idea that he has been 'cheated' by 'nature' or that he is 'unfinished'—are matters of interpretation. While that interpretation of his body may be encouraged by the other characters—their commentary on Richard's disability makes it quite clear that most attitudes toward Richard's embodiment are far from favourable—it is an opinion that Richard has internalized and that he, on some level, chooses to accept and to voice. In Richard's mind, that which is disabled is that which is associated with 'shadow' and 'descant'. Just as the shadow is secondary to light, the descant is secondary to that which is main (it is secondary to the main melodic line). Richard depicts his disability as that which is rendered secondary in comparison to that which is able-bodied or typical.

While generations of historians, scholars, and actors have regarded Richard's body as his destiny, interpreting disability as that which causes villainy, Shakespeare's depiction of Richard's disability is far more ambiguous and subtle than this. Richard is influenced by his cultural moment and by the people around him, but his attitudes toward his disability are ultimately his own. While one could read the line 'I am determinèd to prove a villain' as meaning that Richard is predetermined to do villainy, one can equally well read it as indicating that Richard *feels* that his life is predetermined, and he therefore chooses to undertake villainous acts (*Richard III* 1.1.30).[49] Indeed, as many have pointed out, his courtship of Anne stands in direct contradiction to his statement that he 'cannot prove a lover' because of disability. When he 'woos' Anne successfully, he seems legitimately surprised:

> I do mistake my person all this while.
> Upon my life she finds, although I cannot,
> Myself to be a marv'lous proper man.
> I'll be at charges for a looking-glass
> And entertain a score or two of tailors
> To study fashions to adorn my body.
> Since I am crept in favour with myself,
> I will maintain it with some little cost.
>
> (*Richard III* 1.2.239–46)

Everyone said he couldn't—and until he did, he believed them. Even more tellingly, finding favour with Anne helps Richard to find 'favour with myself'. For Richard, the approval of others seems to translate easily into self-approval.

If Richard hates everybody, including himself, it is not because disability makes one worthy of hate or causes one to hate others. Richard has simply internalized ableist hate. He really believes what he says in the opening soliloquy. In this way, it may be that Richard's villainy is not the result of disability nor of social discrimination against disability but, rather, a self-fulfilling prophecy that results from internalized oppression. Indeed, Richard's interpretation of his own disability appears not only in *Richard III* but also in *3 Henry VI*. Richard describes and interprets his own birth as omen:

> The midwife wondered and the women cried
> 'O, Jesus bless us, he is born with teeth!'—
> And so I was, which plainly signified
> That I should snarl and bite and play the dog.
>
> (*3 Henry VI* 5.6.74–7)

Although Richard says that his mother told him this story, he offers the interpretation of his ominous birth as 'signif[ying]' that he should 'snarl and bite' as his own accepted understanding of what his disability should mean. Richard believes he is 'determinèd' to become a villain because of his disability—and so he becomes one. Thus, Richard motivates his own deviance—not his disability and not social mistreatment—but rather his own internalised belief that the mistreatment is warranted. The fact that the character is able to manifest signs of internalized disability oppression suggests that Shakespeare could imagine disability oppression—and this suggests that, whatever it may have been called at the time, the mistreatment and ostracization of people with disabilities was a recognizable phenomenon in early modern England.

Conclusion: Re-Cripping Richard

One would think that Shakespeare's Richard III is already as crip as they come, the poster child for Shakespeare and disability studies, the obvious place where Shakespeare and disability collide—that we wouldn't have to crip him again. Yet the story of Richard III's history is actually one of disability's erasure. The repeated denial of Richard's disability by historians, by scholars, by popular audiences, and by modern film-makers takes the 'standard-bearer' of disability studies away from scholars, readers, and audience members with disabilities. It symbolically gives Richard III to the able-bodied norm. Even if we hate him (as McRuer notes), hate the villain that Shakespeare presents him as, despise the way that his disability is associated with his villainy, the disability studies approach to Shakespeare that Richard III has come to symbolize is an imperative part of practising inclusive Shakespeare (see Chapter 3). To deny disability studies approaches to Shakespeare is to deny that modern readers, audience members, performers, and scholars with disabilities exist. We should not deny, symbolically or metaphorically or otherwise, the presence of disability and of people with disabilities in the world of Shakespeare. Let's crip Richard and re-crip Richard and re-crip Richard and crip and re-crip Shakespeare studies—in whatever ways we can, as many times as it takes.

2

Making it Accessible

Building Access in Shakespearian Spaces

As performance artist and poet Neil Marcus has famously noted, 'Disability is an art. It is an ingenious way to live.'[1] Impairment is often a source of invention. When the normative method does not work or biological limitations are imposed upon it, circumstances naturally encourage one to invent a new method. For example, I cannot travel alone (the customary method does not work). As a result, I always travel with someone else (we must invent a new method). Over the years, a string of kind volunteers have found themselves cast in the role of disability support person—family members, friends, colleagues, former professors, both former and current students. Some people might find the inability to go places alone to be an obvious deficit—a lack of independence. However, I have often watched the odd unities sparked by my interdependency develop, sometimes unexpectedly, into deep friendships. Not being able to do things alone means that my support people and I have unusual opportunities to do things together. A cultural focus on the potential losses of impairment means that people may not always notice the alternative possibilities impairment creates. The art of creating access, like disability itself, is never simple or one-dimensional. In reality, access is complicated. It is an ongoing process that is never complete. It is the metaphorical point where the creative innovations that spring from disability take place. Disability access can succeed, or it can fail—but I would argue that it can do both in generative and artistic ways that the able-bodied and neurotypical norm all too often overlooks. This holds true for access in Shakespearian spaces: the search for disability

Shakespeare and Disability Studies. Sonya Freeman Loftis, Oxford University Press (2021).
 DOI: 10.1093/oso/9780198864530.003.0003

access to Shakespeare is messy and ongoing but also richly generative and artistic. Common experiences in the classroom teaching of Shakespeare uniquely position Shakespeare scholars and Shakespeare theatres to influence cultural inclusivity at large, and leaders in these areas are creating accommodations that are not just useful but also artistically resonant and subtly revolutionary.

Making Shakespeare Accessible

Over the past two decades, major Shakespeare theatres have become natural leaders in disability accessibility, transforming disability theory into theatrical innovation. This drive for disability access in Shakespearian spaces is motivated in part by Shakespeare's cultural prestige, but, even more importantly, it is a natural outgrowth of Shakespeare's central place in the classroom: the constant search for access is already built into many of the underlying ideological assumptions of Shakespeare studies as a critical field. Indeed, teachers and directors of Shakespeare are already accustomed to thinking about access; we think and talk about access to Shakespeare in terms of social class, financial resources, cultural relatability, educational level, reading ability, and background knowledge. A 400-year-old text is, in some ways, already reduced in its accessibility for modern readers and audiences simply because of time. All teachers are trained to look for barriers between the student and the subject matter and to work on eliminating those barriers; however, this impulse is especially strong for the teacher of Shakespeare. Many high-school and undergraduate students initially find Shakespeare's language daunting, and the Shakespearian mindset, both in and out of the classroom, tends to focus on creating access to texts that popular culture audiences may perceive as dated, highbrow, and difficult to understand. This puts Shakespearians in a natural position to think about disability as another point of potential inaccessibility that ought to be made barrier-free, and this can lead Shakespeare theatres to be trendsetters in matters of disability access.

Indeed, this orientation toward accessibility is so firmly grounded in the Shakespearian mindset that the word 'access' is included in the mission statements of both Shakespeare's Globe and the Royal Shakespeare Company (RSC). The mission of Shakespeare's Globe is to create a 'diverse programme of work' that 'harnesses the power of performance, cultivates intellectual curiosity and excites learning to make Shakespeare accessible for all'.[2] The RSC's mission is 'To inspire and captivate audiences and transform lives through amazing experiences of Shakespeare's plays and of great theatre. Relevant, resonant and accessible, made in Stratford-upon-Avon, shared across the UK and around the world.'[3] Although the writers of such mission statements probably did not specifically intend 'access' to mean 'disability access', it is natural that an emphasis on general accessibility would lead to increased disability awareness—in the wake of the disability rights movement and in the light of the growing neurodiversity movement, the endeavour to create 'access for all' must also include those with physical and mental disabilities. Similarly, the Oregon Shakespeare Festival (OSF) has a mission statement that focuses on a sense of shared humanity, as it seeks to 'reveal our collective humanity through illuminating interpretations of new and classic plays'.[4] Unsurprisingly, these kinds of artistic visions have led Shakespeare theatres such as the Globe, the RSC, and the Oregon Shakespeare Festival to create assisted performances that subtly (and influentially) change what it means for theatre to be accessible.

Although legislation like the Americans with Disabilities Act (ADA 1990) and the UK's Equality Act 2010 have required public venues (including theatres) to adopt more accessible practices for patrons with disabilities, the actual application of new regulations for accessibility is uneven, varying widely from theatre to theatre. In both countries, ways of complying with accessibility standards differ from one venue to the next. Among theatres in the US, the kinds and quality of accommodations offered vary even more widely among individual theatres than they do among theatres in the UK: the Americans with Disabilities Act requires only 'reasonable accommodation', a term that can mean a lot of different things to a lot of different people. For example, some Broadway theatres routinely offer little more than an indication of where wheelchair seating and accessible bathrooms are located. While midsize theatres and large venues in the US usually offer accommodations such as large-print programmes and amplified hearing devices, accommodations such as sign language interpretation, open captioning, audio description, and touch tours—opportunities for blind and low-vision audience members to touch costumes and props before the show—are less common and sometimes only available on an individual basis by advance special request (when they are available at all). 'Sensory-friendly' or 'relaxed' performances (the former term is used in the US, the latter in the UK) are a recent phenomenon. Although they have experienced growing popularity in UK theatres, these types of performances, originally designed for autistic audience members, are still relatively rare in the US. Thus, the variety of accessible performances offered differs widely from one theatre to the next, and there is little to no standardization in how theatres name, describe, or implement various accommodations.

In the face of a lack of standardization, funding, and resources, access managers are constantly placed in a position of invention; what works in one physical space or with one type of show or patron may not work with another—achieving disability access is often a case of try, fail, and try again. In the United States, the John F. Kennedy Center for the Performing Arts has often been considered a gold-standard theatre for disability access: in addition to having beautifully and intelligently designed wheelchair-accessible venues, the Kennedy Center routinely offers sign language interpretation, audio description, open captioning, and sensory-friendly performances. In 2000, the Kennedy Center, working in combination with other American theatres (the Oregon Shakespeare Festival was a founding member), created the Leadership Exchange in Arts and Disability (LEAD), an organization that works to help establish standards for accessible theatre and to educate American theatre practitioners about disability.[5] This work is ongoing, as many theatre practitioners in the US are unaware of LEAD's standards or are unable to implement them due to a lack of funding and resources. Thus, attempts to create accessible theatre, in both the UK and the US, often involve separate theatres making their own individual decisions about access—and even for the laudable team at the Kennedy Center, access is an ongoing learning process as cultural attitudes toward disability and accessibility continually evolve.

Revolutionizing the Relaxed Performance

Both Shakespeare's Globe and the RSC offer relaxed performances on a regular basis, employing techniques that make their relaxed performances more open and accessible than those of many other theatres (including those currently offered at other major theatres such as the Kennedy Center and the National Theatre): the Globe's and the RSC's innovations to the relaxed performance have included imagining relaxed performances for adults, welcoming neurodiverse people at non-relaxed performances, and experimenting with what the RSC has termed 'chilled performance'. Relaxed performances customarily include changes to lighting and sound (to decrease sensory overload), reduced ticket sales (to cut back on crowding), and additional support to prepare audiences for the show (the RSC sends out printed 'visual stories' in advance of relaxed performances, and the RSC and the Globe both offer familiarization tours of the theatre space: these techniques help acclimatize neurodiverse audience members to the sensory space in advance of the performance). Most importantly, relaxed performances offer a theatrical atmosphere that alters the expected social etiquette of the modern audience: actors and staff expect audience members to move around the theatre and to make noise during the performance. Although Shakespeare theatres did not invent the relaxed performance, they have embraced these access opportunities in unique ways. As David Bellwood, access manager at Shakespeare's Globe, jokes: 'all of our performances are relaxed performances.'[6] Not only does performing outdoors under natural light automatically reduce some of the autistic sensory sensitivities introduced by many modern theatre spaces, but a relaxed attitude toward theatre etiquette during regular performances can also go a long way to welcoming neurodiverse audience members. Josefa MacKinnon, assisted performances coordinator at the RSC, agrees that relaxed performances represent a historical return toward a time when theatre etiquette was less rigid: sometimes accessibility means 'changing that etiquette that has been embedded in since Victorian times because it certainly wasn't there in Shakespeare's time'.[7] Relaxed performances can dramatically change the theatre experience of not only neurodiverse people but also neurotypical audience members and actors. Many neurotypical audience members and actors report that they especially enjoy relaxed performances, finding them to be particularly 'freeing': as MacKinnon explains, 'At relaxed performances people laugh more—because you don't feel like you are in such a formal environment—so the laughs are louder or the crying is harder. You feel freer, and you don't have those etiquette restraints.'[8] Relaxed performances encourage encounters between neurotypical and autistic people that affirm autistic ways of being as potentially liberating and generative, finding artistic potential in autistic-influenced social interaction and cultural spaces.

Preparation for this kind of performance can be especially time-consuming for the company, and one of the most important aspects of getting ready for a relaxed performance is educating the actors about neurodiversity. As MacKinnon explains, at the RSC,

> We have to spend three days preparing for a relaxed performance. So that might be going through all the musical and technical elements, working with the actors, any changes... Obviously, relaxed performances aren't a money-making venture for us. We reduce the ticket price, and we never fill them [the auditoriums] out because we like to have 'fidget seats'—is what we call them—so there's enough space between people watching so they can come and go.[9]

However, preparing the actors for a relaxed performance is still one of the most important steps: 'One of the major things we do is talking to the company... to help them understand disability and that helps them to decide if they are going to change anything while they are rehearsing. It also helps them feel calmer about it.'[10] Many neurotypical actors feel nervous about appearing in a relaxed performance, especially if they have never done one before. Abandoning the customary social rules of the theatre space can cause anxiety. MacKinnon finds this fear irrational, since in the theatre,

> Unexpected things happen every night... and it always makes me wonder why people get scared [of relaxed performances]—it is fear of the unknown of what is going to happen during a relaxed performance. 'Oh, my goodness, what if someone makes a noise or what if someone says something to me and what do I do?' Maybe they don't express it, but there is always a little bit of fear. And I always think that people could do that on any night of the week... anything can happen during any live performance.[11]

Since theatrical performance is always, by its very nature, different from night to night, actors may rely on the established social norms of modern theatre-going to introduce some psychological stability into the experience. In the end, MacKinnon reports that the response of the actors is usually very different once they have participated in a relaxed performance: 'What happens when you take all of the rules away? You have more fun. Everybody enjoys them [relaxed performances]—and they will go on to say that they are the best performances they have given. The feedback after the recent relaxed performance of *As You Like It* was just amazing—from the actors and the company and the audience.'[12] Ultimately, actors often discover that appearing in a sensory-friendly performance actually is more relaxed and relaxing than a regular show.

Both the Globe and the RSC offer relaxed performances that differ in subtle ways from what is currently being offered at other theatres. Most significantly, both Shakespeare venues offer relaxed performances that are appropriate for adults. At most theatres, sensory-friendly programmes are designed exclusively for children. The Kennedy Center, frequently regarded as the leading expert on accessible theatre, explains that 'Sensory-friendly performances are designed to create a performing arts experience that is welcoming to all families with children with autism or with other disabilities that create sensory sensitivities.'[13] Thus, all of the Kennedy Center's educational materials for theatre practitioners who want to offer sensory-friendly performances are geared toward performances for children. Their guidebook *Sensory Friendly Programming for People with Social and Cognitive Disabilities* makes no mention of adult audience members with social or cognitive disabilities. This exclusive focus on children is extremely common in autism programmes and resources. Indeed, our culture's tendency to infantilize autistic adults is both common and disturbing: this line of thought is reflected in (and to some extent encouraged by) programmes and resources that address the needs of autistic children without acknowledging the existence of autistic adults.[14] Such materials not only imply that to have autistic traits makes one perpetually childlike but also encourage a lack of resources and programmes designed to address the needs of adults on the autism spectrum. This cultural trend feeds the larger cultural fantasy that autistic children will 'grow out of it' (there is no cure for autism, so there can be no doubt that autistic children will grow up to be autistic adults). Programmes and resources targeted specifically at children also frequently emphasize the needs and voices of neurotypical parents and caregivers rather than those of neurodiverse people. Materials produced by such programmes can, understandably, come across as patronizing to adults with disabilities. For example, I benefit from sensory-friendly performances and accommodations, including visual stories that familiarize people with the sensory space in advance of a visit to a new place. But while the Kennedy Center offers a variety of visual stories on its webpage (the app on the theatre's website that allows one to alter the level and content of the visual story is truly innovative), the most advanced visual story available is written on an elementary-school level, with captions such as 'I will be as quiet as I can be during the show. The show might remind me of happy, excited, sad or scared feelings.'[15] Autistic adults with sensory issues want to be welcomed (and addressed) as adults. The Kennedy Center's exclusive focus on the sensory needs of children also means that sensory-friendly performances are usually only offered for children's shows: for example, the current sensory-friendly offerings at the Kennedy Center are *Halloween Spooktacular* and *Don't Let the Pigeon Drive the Bus (The Musical).* Autistic adults, like neurotypical adults, enjoy seeing adult shows.

Both the RSC and the Globe have revolutionized this infantilizing model, insisting that their relaxed performances and the accommodations they provide should be appropriate for adult audiences. As MacKinnon explains, 'Obviously, our Shakespeare plays are for everyone—we don't change the relaxed performances so that they are geared toward younger audiences at all.'[16] When the RSC first began establishing a quiet room (which they refer to as the 'chill out space') during relaxed performances, MacKinnon had to remind her colleagues to create a space that would be welcoming for adults as well as children: 'I'm very aware that they started off being, "Oh, let's put some crayons and colouring in there and things like that." And I was like "No, we've got to make this not just for kids, this is for everybody!"'[17] Some neurotypical people regard quiet rooms (a place where someone who is experiencing sensory overload can retreat from the noise and crowds) as infantilizing, either assuming that such rooms are only for children or arguing that providing them for adults is catering to an adult in a way that encourages him or her to behave in a childlike fashion. It is important to remember that quiet rooms are not designated for neurotypical adults but rather for neurodiverse ones: the feelings of being overwhelmed that a neurotypical adult may experience in a crowded theatre are not comparable to the disorientation and physical pain that an autistic adult experiences during sensory overload. I still remember being physically ill from sensory overload (and vomiting in the hotel room) after a production of *The Tempest* at the American Shakespeare Center. Not only did the misadventure cause my disability support person a great deal of distress, but it also ensured that the only thing I remember about the production is counting down the final lines of the play in hopes that I would make it out of the theatre in time. Needing a quiet room in response to sensory overload does not make one immature or childlike, and the RSC is to be lauded for providing a quiet room that is 'for everyone'.

The Globe has a similar attitude toward relaxed performance, emphasizing that disability accommodations are provided for neurodiverse adults as well as children. During a relaxed performance, the Globe 'won't make diegetic changes. We aren't going to take things out just because it is a relaxed performance. To us, it is an invitation, to come and to not be judged... We aren't trying to infantilize the audience....'[18] The Globe is now attracting both families with children on the spectrum as well as neurodiverse adults, many of whom are attending typical performances: 'We have more and more neurodivergent people coming to non-relaxed performances. In the past two years, the number of declared neurodivergent people in our audience has tripled.'[19] I would argue that this incredible growth in neurodiverse attendance at the Globe is, in part, a result of the language choices used on the Globe's website. While all of the other theatres that I have surveyed use person-first language when discussing mental and/or neurological disabilities ('person with autism', 'children with autism'), the Globe has decided to use the language of the neurodiversity movement ('neurodiverse', 'neurodivergent') on their website. Language choices in the autism community are hotly contested and politically laden (many parents of autistic children prefer 'person with autism', while the majority of autistic adults prefer 'autistic' or 'neurodiverse'). Using the language of the neurodiversity movement sends a strong message to adults who are involved in that movement ('We are not talking to your parents: we are talking to you'). Because the language choices in their accessibility materials subtly signal acceptance of and support for the neurodiversity movement, it is not surprising that the Globe is attracting more and more neurodiverse audience members.

Because offering relaxed performances often includes education about disability (for both the front-of-house staff and for the actors), relaxed performances, especially those that welcome attendance from adult audiences and from a wide variety of disability communities (not just autistic people), may also be increasing the openness of theatre environments like the RSC and the Globe to having more neurodiverse people attending non-relaxed performances. Although the law states that people with mental and/or neurological disabilities should be equally welcome in all public spaces, that simply is not the lived reality. Relaxed performances are ultimately striving toward inclusion (making theatre accessible to people with mental and/or neurological disabilities), but under the present model this attempt at access also incorporates some exclusion and segregation. While D/deaf audience members and blind audience members are often integrated into the audience for performances that include sign language interpreters, open captioning, or audio description, at many theatres people with mental disabilities may be more likely to attend a separate performance intended especially for them, one that separates them from the 'typical' audience (and unfortunately, at some theatres, neurodiverse people may only feel welcome at such performances if they are children). As Bellwood notes, there is a potential danger of silencing people with disabilities in the attempt to create segregated performances that serve their needs.[20] Theatres in the UK are working to include more neurodiverse audience members in typical shows, a goal which the RSC and Globe have been particularly successful in reaching. As MacKinnon says, 'I very much feel that relaxed performances—they are for everyone. But we also say that anyone can come to any one of our performances. So it's not about having particular performances only available for these types of people or labelling . . . we would do everything possible to try to make you [any audience member] feel comfortable in a performance on any day of the week.'[21] Bellwood agrees, explaining that neurodiverse audience members 'don't need to come to a relaxed performance to enjoy the show'.[22] While relaxed performances are a form of access that may initially seem to foreclose inclusion (by encouraging segregation), they are ultimately fostering a more inclusive theatrical environment overall (by encouraging awareness of and education about disability and, thus, indirectly encouraging theatre companies to welcome neurodiverse people to non-relaxed performances).

The Oregon Shakespeare Festival, like the vast majority of theatres in the US, does not offer relaxed performances (although their accessibility manager hopes to offer some in future seasons). However, their model for the Deaf community is a revolutionary example of how access may both open and foreclose inclusive dramatic practice. The OSF has a strong Deaf following: their website includes videos in sign language that introduce Deaf patrons to the season's shows, and they routinely offer a 'Deaf community weekend' that draws Deaf audiences from around the country. At their sign-language-interpreted performances, the OSF offers 'Deaf community seating': a section of the auditorium that has the best view of the sign language interpreters and has designated seating for Deaf audience members. Julie Simon, Access Services Coordinator at the OSF, describes this seating arrangement, which is simultaneously separate (encouraging members of the Deaf community to sit together and socialize with each other) and inclusive (since Deaf audiences are included at a production where the majority is a hearing audience): 'the interpreted performances have had a positive effect. Even if the [hearing] patrons are not watching the interpreters, they can see that the Deaf community section is filled with people who are fully engaged. Deaf applause is done by waving your hands in the air. So often during an interpreted performance the entire Deaf section will be applauding this way, and I'll look across the theatre and other people will be applauding the same way.'[23] The OSF's inclusion of Deaf audience members as a group that is both separate and yet part of the larger group simultaneously encourages Deaf-community pride (and Deaf-community visibility) while allowing the Deaf community to be at the same performances as the general audience. I look forward to the day when I can sit in neurodiverse-community seating at the theatre (and attend a 'neurodivergent-community weekend'), although I think such innovations may be a long time in coming.

Like any other element of the performance space, disability accommodations made during a relaxed performance can influence the interpretation of Shakespeare's text. For example, the RSC's relaxed performance of *As You Like It* (in 2019) made use of shared lighting during the forest scenes in a way that drew attention to the relaxed nature of the performance space, highlighting the freedom and movement of the audience.[24] The sense that both actors and audience were in the forest of Arden together drew attention to the contrast between court and green world in the play, symbolically juxtaposing the rigid neurotypical conventions of regular theatrical performance (court) with the far less formal and more liberating conventions of autistic social space (Arden).[25] 'Identity' is a key and contested term in the autistic community, since some autistic people can (and do) pass for neurotypical, a passing that sometimes involves a fundamental denial of disabled identity (the decision not to be 'out' as autistic). Thus, the play's emphasis on role playing and identity, in the context of this relaxed performance for the autistic community, could be seen as a commentary on the modern identity politics of autism and on the tensions and controversies inherent in passing for neurotypical. Since relaxed performances offer, at least temporarily, an opportunity to publicly embrace and display neurodiverse identity (there is little or no pressure to pass for neurotypical during a relaxed performance), the relaxed theatre seemed to parallel the forest of Arden, a liberating place in which alternative identities can be freely explored and which encourages the characters of *As You Like It* to express hidden selves that may have been stifled at court.

In other performances, neurodiverse inclusion in non-relaxed theatre settings changes the playing space in ways that bring ambiguity or new meanings to Shakespeare's text. For example, Bellwood describes a performance in which the presence of an audience member with Tourette's fundamentally changed the experience of Shakespeare's *Othello*: 'at the Sam Wanamaker Playhouse I was in the house taking notes . . . and in the audience were two people who were neurodivergent. One had a tic and one had spontaneous language.'[26] Throughout the performance, it was obvious to Bellwood that the audience member with spontaneous language was often on the verge of speaking but holding back. Suddenly and unexpectedly, the woman with Tourette's responded to Iago's direct address to the audience, shouting out, 'You've got to *prove* that Cassio is sleeping with Desdemona!' It was a moment that changed the experience of the play for the entire audience. As Bellwood explains,

She takes the blame, and she flips it—and it comes straight back to Iago who has to respond to that. And the audience came out and was saying, 'that was amazing!' And I'm like, 'Why was it amazing?' Why were these people so excited? Because we already know the play, we know how it ends, we know what he's going to do—but someone literally said it. And he [Iago] had to bring it back, because he asked a question directly to the audience and the audience directly answered and that just gave her [the audience member with Tourette's], that gave the audience, all the power in the play.[27]

This is a story in which accessibility (and inclusion) dramatically altered the theatre experience—in a way that audience members perceived as both surprising and overwhelmingly positive. It is a performance moment that truly bears out the Globe's claim to be 'a democratic space' (a term that appears not only in promotional materials for the theatre but also in its online description of its relaxed performances). We live in a world that greatly devalues the voices of people with mental disabilities. In fact, it is a world that frequently falsely associates mental disability with violence and unreason. During this particular performance, the voice of a neurodivergent person became the voice of reason in a play filled with characters who make ill-considered and irrational mistakes, characters who are inexorably driven toward violent outcomes. In this democratic and inclusive performance, the voice of a neurodiverse person became the most important voice in the play.

The inclusion of both neurotypical and neurodiverse audience members at non-relaxed performances can both alter the artistic experience of the performance and, occasionally, bring ableist assumptions and prejudices to the forefront of discussions of Shakespeare. While able-bodied and neurotypical audience members are usually accepting of accessible-performance practices, they tend to be less tolerant when they find that elements of inclusion or accessibility distract them from the show. For example, Bellwood remembers receiving particularly virulent complaints from one individual regarding neurodiverse audience members with Tourette's who attended a production of *Much Ado about Nothing*:

One person complained, saying it was really wrong of us to sell them tickets, saying, 'You can't sell tickets to people with Tourette's.' I said, 'That's breaking the law!' He was trying to coerce me into breaking the law and . . . it opened the conversation for him about his assumptions about Tourette's . . . he said, 'They couldn't possibly have understood the play.' Two of them are writers and one of them is an avid reader of Shakespeare's works—and I'm thinking, 'these guys know more about Shakespeare than you do.'[28]

Such audience complaints point to a number of underlying ideological assumptions about disability and Shakespeare. Because the neurodiverse audience members interrupted the normal etiquette of the theatre event with verbal tics, the neurotypical audience member at this (non-relaxed) performance was upset and offended. His belief that people with disabilities should naturally be excluded from some spaces (in spite of the law's assertion that they should have equality) is built on the assumption that exclusion is natural and to the benefit of able-bodied people (verbal tics can be distracting to other audience members) but also on the idea that neurodiverse people are not capable of understanding Shakespeare's works. In the audience member's response, Shakespeare becomes a contested symbol of cognitive ability, as the complaint implies both that Shakespeare should be purely the realm of the neurotypical and able-bodied ('You can't sell tickets to people with Tourette's') and that this exclusion is natural, already built into the minds of those who are neurodiverse ('They couldn't possibly have understood the play'). In such prejudicial assumptions, to understand Shakespeare becomes a marker of cognitive ability—appreciating Shakespeare is taken as proof of neurotypicality, while the inability to understand Shakespeare is falsely associated with the disabled mind. Thus, the assumed 'able-bodied' Shakespeare—and the ownership of his words—is sometimes claimed by the able-bodied as a marker of that which is normative.

Indeed, the desire to claim the presumed 'able-bodied Shakespeare' as the symbol of an idealized able-bodied norm includes not only considerations of neurodiversity but also other kinds of accommodations. Sometimes audience responses to accessibility suggest both ableist hostility and a sense of claiming knowledge of Shakespeare as the marker of intellectual ability that people with disabilities (any of kind of disability) are assumed not to have. Under such schemas, to understand Shakespeare and appreciate his works in a specific way is to emphasize a particular kind of ability that is falsely prioritized as a marker of intelligence and taste in our educational system. For instance, some able-bodied audience members (and even some audience members with disabilities) are unaware of what kinds of disability accommodations are available and may sometimes misinterpret the presence of such accommodations. On one occasion, Bellwood received a very unusual complaint about one of the Globe's open-captioned performances: 'We did get an email once from a man complaining about the captions—that he found them patronizing. He said, "I don't need you to write the text on the wall. I understand it anyway." He didn't understand what we were trying to achieve.'[29] The failure to recognize that 'invisible' disability exists is an all-too-common phenomenon. In this case, the audience member was completely unaware of the presence of D/deaf, hard-of-hearing, and/or neurodiverse audience members who benefited from the open captioning. Even more tellingly, he interpreted the efforts to provide accommodations for such audience members as a reduction of the Shakespearian text's intellectual challenge, with the accompanying assumption that an educated person can always understand Shakespeare's language aurally. The oralist assumption that prioritizes spoken language over signed, written, or typed speech is one that is used to exclude and discredit Deaf people as well as neurodiverse people who type to communicate. In this case, the audience member believed that there is only one way to prove knowledge of Shakespeare (read: ability, education, artistic discernment)—to apprehend and understand Shakespeare's words when they are spoken aloud.

Indeed, the fear that altering Shakespeare's text for those with disabilities will somehow necessitate a diluting of Shakespeare's intellectual content is a common (and totally unnecessary and often implicitly ableist) fear about making disability accommodations. For example, in considering relaxed performances some artistic directors may initially express hesitation, worried that changes to the play may somehow detract from their artistic vision of the work. In truth, most plays can be adapted for relaxed performance with no changes to the actual script, and it is possible to offer the 'relaxed' atmosphere of the auditorium even without making sensory changes to the production. For example, the RSC has recently been experimenting with 'chilled performances', in which the freeing atmosphere of relaxed performances is offered (allowing people to move around and in and out of the auditorium, talk among themselves, and so on) without the sensory changes usually made during a relaxed performance specifically designed for people with sensory sensitivities. Such performances have proven popular for elderly patrons with dementia and their families, parents with babes in arms, and other theatregoers who, for whatever reason, benefit from less formal etiquette in the auditorium.

The appeal of chilled performances for certain able-bodied audience members (such as those who serve as caregivers for an elderly parent or a small child) is a reminder that thinking accessibly can benefit a wide variety of different people—not just people with disabilities. In fact, captioned performances of Shakespeare's works, at both the Globe and at the OSF, have become popular for audience members for whom English is a second language. After having largely negative experiences with their open-captioning system (ranging from technology problems to complaints from able-bodied audience members who found the captioning distracting), the OSF switched to captioning on individual tablets placed on a stand in front of each patron who requested it, a system that has achieved enormous success and has been in high demand. As Simon explains, 'Every so often someone who is not using the captions will lean over to the person who is and find that they like it, especially during Shakespeare, because it helps them with the language . . . often we will get a request from a patron who is a non-native English speaker who uses the tablet as a back-up to help them with the play.'[30] Unlike the Globe spectator who was offended by the 'writing on the wall', once OSF patrons began to realize that captioning was available, some able-bodied audience members discovered that they could also benefit from it. Thus, revolutionizing the relaxed performance—imagining relaxed performances for adults, welcoming neurodiverse people at typical performances, and creating a 'chilled performance' that is also beneficial for some able-bodied audience members—is part of a larger trend in which accessibility in the arts can benefit all of us—neurodiverse, neurotypical, disabled, and able-bodied alike.

One Hundred Per Cent Accessible?: Best Practices for Accessible Theatre

There are a variety of practical steps that even small theatres can take to improve accessibility. But in taking such steps, it is important to acknowledge that accessibility is always a work in progress, never a static end goal that can be achieved. As a person with impairments that are particularly difficult to accommodate, I am always troubled by websites that proclaim that an event will be '100 per cent accessible' or 'inclusive'. Such claims often sound insincere to people with disabilities, as no event can ever truly fulfil the promise. Universal design (making everything accessible all of the time) is theoretically appealing but practically impossible. For example, accommodating one disability community may conflict with the accommodations needed by another individual or group. Bellwood recalls a performance at the Globe in which the attempt at access became simultaneously both access and exclusion: 'there can be a clash between different disabled people... last year we had an actress, she signed... and we had a blind audience member, and he just liked listening to Shakespeare's language. He said the trouble was that we took that away from him. So in making the stage accessible to the Deaf actor we took something away from the blind audience member.'[31] Even theatres that are highly accessible are rarely able to fully employ universal design. The Globe, the RSC, and the OSF, like many theatres, use a system in which individual patrons self-identify as disabled and request accommodations (or book tickets to performances that are specifically marked as providing accommodations). There are obvious limitations to such systems: it puts the burden of arranging accommodations on the individual needing accommodations (it creates more logistical work for patrons with disabilities), as well as limiting the number of performances (and sometimes seating options) available for audience members with certain impairments. The true fulfilment of universal design would be a performance in which all possible needed accommodations are provided simultaneously—without individuals having to request any alterations to the environment or programme. However, the funding and resources required to make every performance at every theatre completely accessible are not realistically available. Because of a lack of funding and resources, as well as the challenges of conflicting access needs, offering individual accommodations upon request (or assisted performances that audience members with disabilities can choose to attend) is often the only possible method for creating accessible theatre. Even if the resources are available, and it is possible to make the building wheelchair-accessible, to provide sign language interpreters, to offer audio description and a touch tour, to 'relax' the performance space, and to offer those accommodations simultaneously at every performance or event, access is not always about physical spaces and communicative logistics (although those aspects of access are important).

Programmes that claim to be '100 per cent accessible' are sometimes overlooking the fact that access includes intellectual content and social spaces. For example, the programme may include material that is not equally understandable for an audience member with an intellectual disability. In addition, it is difficult (if not impossible) for organizers of an event to ensure that both employees of the organization and participants from the general public will equally include autistic people in social aspects of a given gathering. For instance, the Society for Disability Studies long worked to offer a professional conference that followed the theory of universal design—and it was the most joyously accessible conference I have ever attended. Each conference panel had a sign language interpreter and live captioning. Longer gaps between events allowed time for those with pain and fatigue to rest between panels. A quiet room was set aside for neurodiverse attendees who needed to get out of the crowd (although, to clarify, there was a still quite a crowd). But in spite of the laudable strides made by the Society in attempting to achieve universal design, the conference was never one hundred per cent accessible (nor, wisely, did it ever claim to be). For example, if neurodiverse attendees are not invited (or are not able) to socialize and network with their colleagues in the crowded restaurants and bars after the panels, the conference—and the professional networking opportunities it offers to the neurotypical—were never fully accessible to them. In this case, full inclusion for autistic colleagues might include a change of venue (deliberately choosing to socialize after hours in a place that is neither crowded nor noisy) as well as a fundamental change in the social expectations established for professional networking (successful neurodiverse/neurotypical social interactions can require patience, flexibility, and open-mindedness—from both parties). Full inclusion for people with intellectual, social, and communication disabilities requires a change of cultural attitudes and social norms, and sometimes these kinds of accommodations, while invisible and intangible, are some of the most challenging to make. While autistic people form one of the groups most likely to experience social exclusion (even at gatherings of people with disabilities), that doesn't mean that D/deaf people, blind people, or people using wheelchairs may not experience social exclusion because of communication difficulties, social stigma, or inaccessible spaces—people may be socially excluded because of a wide variety of visible or invisible impairments.

At other times, physical access may be influenced by factors that are largely (or completely) outside of the theatre's control. For example, if the performance is in a city that has public transportation that is difficult for people with certain impairments to access, some people with disabilities will be prevented from attending the 'accessible' theatre before they even get there. (While this realization might encourage people to lobby for changes in a city's public transport system, it may take a long time to make such changes.) Destination theatres can only be a destination for those who are able to travel to them (and the challenges of travel, for people with a wide variety of different impairments, are notorious). In the end, it will always be possible to think of someone whose particular disability will cause them to be excluded. Will someone who is in hospital undergoing surgery be able to attend the event? If not, it is not '100 per cent accessible'. Even when events can be live-streamed on the internet, such programmes and events will still face accessibility challenges: does the streaming performance include sign language interpretation, live captioning, and audio description for blind audience members?; does an online virtual meeting use technology that includes fast-paced or flashing images that may cause sensory overload for neurodiverse participants? There can be no doubt that the strides toward access and inclusion that people make in working toward universal design are worthwhile, but it is imperative to acknowledge that total access has not been (and may never be) achieved by any programme, location, or event.

Thus, when talking about accessibility, theatres should use language that signals the messy work in progress that is access: 'this theatre strives to achieve universal design' or 'this theatre works to be as accessible as possible'. Then, those in positions of leadership at theatres should honestly strive to achieve universal design and work to be as accessible as possible—with the knowledge that each attempt will make a difference in the lives of people with disabilities but also with the knowledge that universal design may be an unreachable goal. The RSC's statement on their accessibility webpage is a good example of this kind of acknowledgement: 'We want everything we do to be accessible to all our audiences and are looking for ways to break down barriers so more people can enjoy theatre at its best.'[32] Rather than claiming that it has mastered accessibility, the RSC acknowledges that it *wants* its theatre to be accessible, and it seeks feedback on ways to become even more accessible (it is 'looking for ways to break down barriers'). In line with theories regarding universal design, both the Globe and RSC websites indicate that accessibility is a project that is always in the works rather than an end goal that has already been achieved.

Acknowledging that access is always a work in progress that will need constant improvement, and given that the motto of the disability rights movement is 'nothing about us without us', it is imperative that programmes for people with disabilities seek input and feedback from those audiences the programme is designed to reach. Ideally, people with disabilities should hold planning and leadership roles in organizations that wish to reach audience members with disabilities. Ableist assumptions often mean that little effort is exerted to hire people with disabilities in leadership roles. For example, some organizations perceive people with intellectual, learning, or developmental disabilities as being unable to contribute leadership to programmes designed for those populations. This is untrue: there are many college graduates with intellectual, learning, and/or developmental disabilities who are either unemployed or underemployed. The best programmes for people with disabilities include people from the disability community and openly invite comments from patrons with disabilities. As MacKinnon advises, 'it is always about going back to the [disability] community and getting their feedback the whole time . . . Have the people in the room who you are making it for. Keep the conversations going.'[33] There are lots of ways to do this successfully, but creating a webpage devoted to disability access, and using welcoming language on it, is a good place to start. For example, the Globe's access page states that 'we aim to be as welcoming and inclusive as possible. We believe that equal access can only be achieved with your input, so please let us know if you feel there is anything we can do to improve your visit.'[34] While this might seem like a common-sense suggestion, many theatres in the US neither have a part of their web presence devoted to access nor make a public effort to seek feedback from the disability community.

Theatres should try to make their access plans easy to understand and easy to use. Good communication is key: it is helpful to list 'access' on the theatre's website in a place where it is easy to find from the main page. (How prominently a theatre lists 'access' says a lot to audience members with disabilities about how much they value it.) On the Globe and RSC main websites, 'Access' is easy to find at the top of the page; on the Globe's 'plan your visit' page, 'Access' is a large and colourful button taking up about a fifth of the page. This kind of prominent placement sends a strong message to the disability community. It is also important to offer both an email address and phone number where someone who can help with accessibility can be easily reached (some disabilities will make it more difficult to communicate by either phone or email, so it is very helpful to include both options). Making it clear exactly what kinds of accommodations a theatre offers and making those accommodations easy to request are a huge draw for audience members with disabilities, who are often used to fighting and struggling to get the accommodations they need. The RSC offers a variety of videos on their access webpage, each geared toward a specific disability community, explaining the kinds of accommodations they offer. The Globe has a section of their 'accessibility scheme' in which audience members can check boxes from a detailed list of possible accommodations: the list takes in a wide variety of possible access needs including a reduced price ticket for a companion (50 per cent off for the person with a disability and 50 per cent off for the companion, so people with disabilities avoid the all-too-common problem of having to pay twice as much because they need one-on-one support), ability to request an aisle seat, touch tours, audio-described performance, hearing loop, captioned performance, sign-language-interpreted performance, wheelchair-accessible seating, and more. The Globe's form is extremely helpful because the options (even ones that were once considered unusual, like 'companion') are listed; although the patron must self-identify as disabled to use the form, there is no pressure to 'invent' and describe what the patron needs or to explain why they need it (a common roadblock I encounter in inaccessible spaces).

Another aspect of good communication involves language choices. Theatres that use up-to-date terminology regarding disability on their websites will inevitably come across as more welcoming. The terms in use are ever-shifting, but at the time of writing the most up-to-date terminology includes audience members with disabilities, audience members who use wheelchairs, D/deaf audience members, audience members who are hard of hearing, blind audience members, audience members with low vision, and neurodiverse/neurodivergent audience members. It is important to remember that many Deaf people do not self-identify as disabled (since they speak sign language, they self-identify as a linguistic minority group). Thus, access plans should be designed for 'Deaf people and people with disabilities'. Currently, most theatres in the US offer no accommodations for neurodivergent people. If a theatre is interested in offering accommodations for neurodivergent audience members, they might consider offering a discounted companion ticket and an aisle seat for neurodivergent audience members upon request (some neurodiverse people cannot go to the theatre by themselves and many need extra personal space); establishing a quiet room in the theatre where audience members can go in case of sensory overload; including a sensory warning on the theatre's website for shows that use flashing lights or startling, loud sound effects; and including a warning for violent content that might be triggering for people with post-traumatic stress disorder. All of these are small changes (changes to website design or offering accommodations that are low-cost, such as a quiet room) that could make theatre companies and their performances more accessible.[35]

Sometimes good accessibility is about attitude, about offering hospitality in ways that run counter to all-too-common experiences of ableism. Indeed, it is possible that many able-bodied and neurotypical people underestimate how dehumanizing (and how common) ableist discrimination can be. For example, people who realize that I have a developmental disability routinely assume that my husband is my caregiver. Strangers off-campus do not always address me as an equal (or even as an adult). Where knowledge of my disability identity precedes me, the assumption that I am not capable of understanding, communicating, or making decisions for myself is a common occurrence. The experience of this kind of ableism is shared by many people across all different kinds of disability communities. Thus, it is not surprising that many people with disabilities emphasize and prioritize the attitude with which access is offered rather than simply considering the logistics of access. As disability theorist Leah Piepzna-Samarasinha argues, 'When access is centralized at the beginning dream of every action or event, that is radical love. I mean that access is far more to me than a checklist of accessibility needs—though checklists are needed and necessary. I mean that without deep love and care for each other . . . an event can have all the fragrance-free soap and interpreters and thirty-six-inch-wide doorways in the world. And it can still be empty.'[36] As Piepzna-Samarasinha points out, logistical access can fail to achieve real inclusion when it does not signal an attempt to change the larger ableist attitudes that affect disability communities.

Thus, when people with disabilities say that access at theatres can be an emotional, validating, and humanizing experience, they are not engaging in hyperbole. For example, Joanna Wood, a blind audience member at Shakespeare's Globe, explains that 'The power of audio description is how you're treated . . . at the Sam Wanamaker Playhouse I was treated like a human . . . A full person, someone with value and worth . . . Because a stranger, someone who doesn't know you, who is meeting you for the first time . . . sees you as a person, treats you as a person . . . this is more than transformative . . . .'[37] Being treated as an equal by strangers is often an able-bodied privilege. Thus, Wood was moved not just by the access offered at the Globe but also by the attitude with which it was offered. Wood is not alone in her perception that attitudes at the Globe run counter to common cultural discourses about disability:

> I've certainly met others on touch tours since who share my sense that the power of audio description is as much to do with the people you encounter and their attitude as the performance itself. This goes so far beyond an equal right of access or even the power of theatre as an art form. And I don't think that . . . theatres and theatre people realise that in this, in these moments, in these encounters, they're doing something extraordinary that other places in society, in life, simply aren't.[38]

In reviewing the Globe, the RSC, and the OSF, patrons with disabilities emphasize a sense of welcome and hospitality. Claire

Szabo-Cassella, who uses a wheelchair and is a regular attendee at the OSF, explains:

> I have often teared up at the theater, but at the Oregon Shakespeare Festival, I teared up *because* of the theater. Let me explain: OSF's dedication to access for all its patrons is an impressive example of social responsibility . . . what got me all choked up was . . . The seating diagram for the Angus Bowmer Theatre showed that extra room had been created to accommodate people utilizing mobility devices, people like me, and with a good number of companion seats. A dozen or more seats . . . were taken out in order to widen two aisles specifically for wheelchair seating.[39]

While the physical logistics of access at the theatre (the theatre's decision to remove seats, and thus to reduce ticket sales, to make more room for wheelchair users) was moving for Szabo-Cassella, she also comments on the access intimacy she experienced with people at the theatre.

'Access intimacy' is the ability to anticipate the needs of someone with a disability without being told about those needs in advance.[40] Describing the OSF as 'gracious hosts', Cassella explains that theatre staff were able to understand her needs as a person who uses a wheelchair: 'Inside and outside the theatres, these red-vested stewards of the OSF theatre experience (many of them volunteers) have always made us feel so welcome . . . The entire team of OSF ushers have often anticipated our accessibility needs before we have.'[41] Thus, patrons with disabilities talk about these theatres and their accommodations in terms that consider equity and social justice; but they also emphasize the powerful emotional impact of successful access. Although the experience of access intimacy can be moving and validating, we only achieve such intimacy by continually listening to, and seeking to learn from, each other. Disability theorist Mia Mingus warns against 'treat [ing] access as a logistical interaction, rather than a human interaction'.[42] Kelsie Acton and her co-authors emphasize the human and emotional connection of hospitality that is made in giving and receiving disability accommodations by describing access as an act of 'being in relationship'.[43] Ultimately, access is best achieved when theatres and programmes work in close relationship with the disability communities they seek to serve, constantly striving to offer accessibility in a spirit of hospitality, equality, and shared humanity.

The Art of Access

Creating access changes people's *minds*. It changes conceptions about which bodies and minds are normative; it changes stereotypes about where people with disabilities can go and what they can do; it changes mistaken conceptions about what people with disabilities are able to know and to understand. In the case of encounters with Shakespeare, working toward accessibility means that major Shakespeare theatres have taken on a responsibility not just to educate the public about the works of William Shakespeare but also, by extension, to educate them about disability and disability rights. Preparing actors for a relaxed performance includes increasing autism awareness for the entire theatre company. Fielding complaints from audience members who believe that neurodiverse people cannot understand the show means confronting (and correcting) beliefs that Shakespeare belongs exclusively to able-bodied and neurotypical people. Working toward theatre that is truly inclusive for neurodiverse audiences means changing conceptions that cast Shakespeare as the symbol of 'normative' intellectual ability by reminding audiences that 'intellectual ability' can include a wide variety of diverse ways to communicate and to understand. The belief in Shakespeare's universality (further explored in Chapter 3), may encourage access in a positive way in Shakespearian spaces: the notion that 'Shakespeare is for everyone' (a common phrase at the Globe) is a self-fulfilling prophecy of sorts. Whether Shakespeare really is for everyone—or not—is irrelevant. What matters is that many theatre practitioners are moved to try to make him so.

In the end, disability access to Shakespeare's works can be about both artistry and social justice. As Bellwood explains,

> There is a fine and very blurry line between access and art . . . Theatre gives us an opportunity . . . in a way that more corporate structures or the more medical model of thinking would not. There are aspects of access that definitely are art. Sign language, for example, and the interpretation of Shakespeare into sign language, has artistry to it. Audio description has artistry to it . . . And what matters is whether or not theatre professionals are on board with that being a part of their creative output or whether they see it as accommodations, as just a part of the system.

In some ways, thinking of accessibility as a part of the art of Shakespeare, as a part of the vision of a theatrical performance from the very beginning of its creation, speaks to Leah Piepzna-Samarasinha's belief that prioritizing access is 'radical love'. It means imagining for and preparing for an inclusive world—even if that world hasn't arrived yet. It means recognizing the ways in which disability experience can be liberating and inventive (as in a relaxed performance). It means recognizing that disability access (and the experience of Shakespeare) is not something that is given by able-bodied people to people with disabilities but, rather, a work of social justice that communities of diverse people build and create together. As Bellwood puts it, 'People say, "The Globe is doing nice things." But this [access] isn't charity. This is human rights.'[44]

3

Play for All

Shakespeare Therapy and the Concept of Inclusion

In the autumn of 2019, I saw a performance of *Descent* by Kinetic Light, a group of disabled artists who set out to make their show as accessible as possible. It had been a hard week for me, so my support person and I arrived at the theatre very early ('I want to take my time,' I told her). By 'take my time' I meant that I wanted to move so slowly that maybe I would not get physically sick from the crowd and the noise. Autistic people are often left out of the accommodation process, even in those spaces that excel in providing quality accommodations for people with physical disabilities. Most theatres do not have a quiet room for people who get sensory overload from the crowd and the noise—and in the ones that do, it is usually a reappropriated broom cupboard. The artistic director of Kinetic Light, Alice Sheppard, had already told me that a quiet room would be available before the show and during the intermission. However, when I arrived at Georgia Tech's Ferst Center for the Arts, I was surprised and delighted to be escorted out of the theatre and into the closed student centre next door. My support person and I would have been very grateful for a quiet room. Instead, we found ourselves in an entire quiet building, complete with quiet bathrooms. On top of that, the Ferst Center's Patron and Event Services Coordinator personally ushered us from the quiet space to our seats ten minutes before the show and came back at the intermission to lead us back to the empty student centre. It was the first time in my life that I ever attended a theatre and left the performance without any sensory overload or physical pain.

Shakespeare and Disability Studies. Sonya Freeman Loftis, Oxford University Press (2021).
 DOI: 10.1093/oso/9780198864530.003.0004

The next day, I tried to tell one of my students about the performance. 'I had an entire quiet building! It was amazing!' I exclaimed. 'But you aren't telling me about the performance, Dr Loftis,' he said in the very patient voice that neurotypical people use when autistic people are talking off topic; 'you are only telling me about the accommodations.' 'The performance', I responded, 'was aesthetically radical. . . .' But even as I told him about *Descent*, about how Alice Sheppard and Laurel Lawson had plunged in their wheelchairs across a giant and sinuously curving ramp, moving with a majesty and beauty that showcased disability as a powerful aesthetic, I knew that I had failed to clearly explain to my student the lesson that I wanted to teach him about this performance. As Sheppard explains, 'Kinetic Light is committed to access as being an integral part of our works, not a secondary accommodation. We invite artists and cultural works to think of access as an aesthetic.'[1] There is something beautiful about not being relegated to the broom cupboard, about sitting on the couches in the empty student centre in perfect silence before the show. There is something beautiful about the graceful dance of being ushered back and forth from the autistic quiet into the neurotypical noise of the theatre. There is something beautiful about being anticipated in advance, about participating without pain. Although I tried my best to explain, my able-bodied student did not understand that the disability accommodations were a part of the performance.

I left Kinetic Light's *Descent* feeling included, a rare event that reminded me of how very seldom I feel that way. Inclusion is a goal that many programmes strive to reach, but as a concept it is hard to define. In general, theatrical performances and programmes which are 'inclusive' are welcoming to and accepting of people with diverse backgrounds, bodies, and minds. But while inclusion is a desirable goal, encouraging social justice, equity, and diversity, inclusion can be difficult to achieve. Paradoxically, I felt most included by Kinetic Light when I was excluded (literally ushered to another building). Inclusion may sometimes be a state of mind (Kinetic Light anticipated the needs of an autistic audience member) or maybe even an emotion (I felt included, even when I was physically separated from the rest of the audience). Inclusion is a complicated goal, an endeavour that starts at the level of language and thoughts and theory, progressing, as the chapters in this book do, from theory, through access, to inclusion.

Part of the thesis of this book is that real inclusion for people with disabilities cannot exist without access and that quality access is almost always informed by and grounded in disability theory.

If we understand 'inclusive Shakespeare' as those programmes and performances that attempt to meet the access needs of diverse audiences, to make diverse audiences feel a part of the practice and performance of Shakespeare, we will inevitably meet many challenges in our attempts to create inclusive Shakespeare. One challenge is the difficulty, particularly as it pertains to audience members with mental disabilities who engage with Shakespeare, of finding ways for organizers, practitioners, and participants to understand and work through the complex ideological problems that may arise in Shakespeare therapy programmes. Another is the failure of universal design and the way in which universal design may become bound up with notions about 'universal' Shakespeare. While some Shakespeare therapy programmes foster true access and inclusion for people with mental disabilities, others do not. In this chapter, I focus on two Shakespeare therapy programmes: Stephan Wolfert's DE-CRUIT (a Shakespeare-based therapy for war veterans with post-traumatic stress disorder) and Kelly Hunter's Hunter Heartbeat Method (HHM, a Shakespeare-based therapy for autistic children). Both are Shakespeare therapy programmes designed explicitly for people with mental disabilities. While many Shakespeare therapy programmes strive to break away from the medical model of disability and to provide access and inclusion for people with disabilities, some are more successful in achieving those goals than others. Indeed, some Shakespeare therapy programmes may ironically replicate and reinforce the medical model of disability while inadvertently discouraging access and inclusion.

Shakespeare Therapy outside of the Medical Model: DE-CRUIT

Stephan Wolfert's DE-CRUIT, a programme designed for veterans with post-traumatic stress disorder (PTSD), differs from most other Shakespeare therapy programmes in key ways: the DE-CRUIT programme is focused on building and fostering disability community, and it encourages participants to appropriate and rewrite Shakespeare's works in ways that speak to their lived experience of disability. Stephan Wolfert, a veteran who has PTSD, created and runs the DE-CRUIT programme, and he works to create a sense of disability community among participants. In this way, DE-CRUIT runs counter to the medical model of disability. The medical model is based on a clear power hierarchy: physicians and psychiatrists give treatment, and patients receive treatment. According to the medical model, medical professionals offer diagnosis, describe disabilities, and offer therapies; the narrative about disability and, by extension, people with disabilities is created by medical authorities. This medical discourse is sometimes disempowering for people with disabilities, since, under the medical model, people with disabilities are often not regarded as being an 'authority' on their disability or as having the authority to tell narratives about their own experiences. Thus, the lived experience of people with disabilities is often devalued, either implicitly or explicitly, under the medical model. By de-emphasizing disability as pathology, the social model runs counter to this, allowing more agency and voice for people with disabilities. The social model encourages people with disabilities to tell their own stories, creating spaces for people with disabilities to make their own communities and to help other people in their disability community by offering shared experiences and support.

DE-CRUIT encapsulates the social model, no doubt in part because it is a programme in which people with disabilities have leadership roles. In DE-CRUIT, people who have PTSD share their experiences and help other people who have PTSD. As Drew Wiggins explains, DE-CRUIT represents 'a radical departure from conventional care' because when participants

> are viewed through this [the medical] lens, the trauma that veterans may have experienced—and the difficulties they may be having returning to civilian life—are identified as a 'pathology' that resides within the individual... DE-CRUIT provides a radical alternative to that medical approach. Veterans are understood to be suffering from what might be described as a failure to re-integrate into civilian society. They come back from war and they feel *they don't fit in.*[2]

The emphasis here is on society: veterans who have experienced trauma may feel that 'they don't fit in' to civilian social structures. DE-CRUIT acknowledges that people with disabilities are not the problem, encouraging participants to see that 'The problem wasn't solely within them; it resided in their relationship to the civilian world'. Thus, DE-CRUIT focuses on helping people who have PTSD to share their traumas with other people who have PTSD and on encouraging veterans to create a sense of disability community. The feeling of fitting in with one's own disability community may help to ease the discomfort of feeling that one does not fit in with neurotypical people. As Wolfert explains his programme to other veterans, 'This is where you can find community to help you.' As they stand together in a circle, Wolfert encourages participants to 'Know that this is the group of people that you can think about this week if we start to feel lost or lonely'. Craig Manbauman, a participant in the programme, explains that this focus on community was extremely important to him: 'Although some traumas happen in isolation, to think that the healing must happen in isolation is a fallacy... You need that societal space for healing and validation, to see you through it and know that you are supported.' Because of this focus on disability community, the programme is extremely responsive to the needs of veterans: 'As Wolfert designed the DE-CRUIT programme, with support from [Alisha] Ali and others, he constantly focused on this question: What did veterans say they needed? They told of three overarching needs: "I need to get a job; I need to relate to people around me; I need community".' In this way, DE-CRUIT fosters and encourages disability community.

Second, DE-CRUIT represents an appropriation of Shakespeare's text created by and for a specific disability community: DE-CRUIT changes Shakespeare in order for the playwright's text to be manipulated and used specifically by veterans with PTSD in a way that is unique to their disability experiences. Wolfert's story is one of someone with a disability discovering that Shakespeare's work spoke to an aspect of his disability experience. According to Wolfert, 'among the characters in Shakespeare's plays, there are numerous veterans who astutely describe their military trauma'. Thus, he began appropriating and using Shakespeare's words in a way that helped him to express his experience of disability, creating a one-man show called *Cry Havoc!* Wolfert built on this work in the DE-CRUIT programme, empowering veterans to adapt Shakespeare's text in ways that help them to communicate their own experiences of trauma to other members of their disability community.

Thus, the emphasis is not on learning Shakespeare but, rather, on rewriting Shakespeare, on appropriating his words and themes. As Manbauman explains, the programme is not about an 'obligation to know Shakespeare' but, rather, Wolfert encourages participants to 'make yourself present for the words and dare to be wrong'. This appropriation allows members of a particular disability community to use Shakespeare's words to voice and share disability experiences with each other. According to Wiggins, DE-CRUIT participants create their own 'trauma monologue' that reflects their unique experience of trauma: then the veteran's monologue is paired with a speech from Shakespeare that has related themes, and the veteran is given group support and help as he or she prepares and performs both monologues. As Alisha Ali, a researcher who has worked alongside Wolfert, explains, 'We now can categorize the themes like insomnia, moral injury, sense of betrayal, etc., and in those categories there are monologues from Shakespeare that fit within that . . . For example, someone with recurring nightmares might be given *Richard III* or the infamous "Out, Damned Spot" monologue of Lady Macbeth.' In pairing personal monologues with passages from Shakespeare, DE-CRUIT allows the disability community to appropriate Shakespeare's cultural authority. Thus, the programme encourages veterans to rewrite Shakespeare's words in order to voice a marginalized life experience that is often ignored in mainstream culture. As the words of the veterans are presented alongside the soliloquies of Shakespeare, their disability narratives, and their own created texts, are given equal weight with those of Shakespeare.

While these major differences distinguish the programme from many other Shakespeare therapy programmes, there are commonalities between DE-CRUIT (which has been proven to reduce the symptoms associated with PTSD in adults) and Kelly Hunter's Hunter Heartbeat Method (which has been proven to encourage neurotypical behaviour in autistic children). Both programmes begin sessions with participants forming a circle and making eye contact with others. While this practice is not dictated by any specific Shakespeare plays, it may tap into the sense of community created by a troupe of actors performing theatre together. In the beginning ritual for each therapy programme, participants are encouraged to connect with other people in the circle (by making eye contact) and also to express their feelings. Wolfert encourages DE-CRUIT participants to 'Check in with yourself', asking them to share their feelings with each other: 'Let's go around the circle...My name is...and right now I feel....' When forming a circle in the beginning of Hunter Heartbeat Method sessions, autistic children express emotion by making faces that show different feelings (happiness, sadness, and anger).[3] Thus, the opening logistics of the two programmes are quite similar.

Such activities may remind us that Shakespeare therapy is a subset of theatre as therapy. Theatre may encourage well-being in human beings for a variety of reasons: because it encourages community, because it allows one to express emotion, because performing a play may encourage a feeling of success, and because theatre can be fun. In which case, theatre might be beneficial for many people—not just for people with disabilities. The opening circle activity of these therapies also suggests that engaging with the works of another playwright might be just as beneficial as engaging with the works of Shakespeare. Shakespearian plays are not the only kind of theatre that can encourage community, allow one to express emotion, foster a feeling of success, and offer a chance to have fun. Because Shakespeare's verse is reputed to be particularly challenging, however, people may feel a special sense of accomplishment in performing Shakespeare, as opposed to performing the work of a less well-known author.[4] Like many Shakespeare therapy programmes, DE-CRUIT often culminates in a public performance. Wiggins notes that 'as any stage actor can attest, the aftermath of a public performance provides an actor with a sense of accomplishment and competence, and the joy of having done so as part of a troupe'. As Wiggins explains, Ali's research has shown that DE-CRUIT 'produces "significant increases in self-efficacy", which means participants gain a greater belief in their own "abilities and competencies"' by participating in the programme. In other words, popular culture beliefs that Shakespeare is particularly challenging may mean that those who perform Shakespeare increase 'self-efficacy' more than they might if they chose another playwright. As Wiggins explains, Wolfert selected Shakespeare for his programme because he saw Shakespeare's veteran characters as expressing sentiments and experiences that were similar to his own experiences as a veteran. However, many Shakespeare therapy programmes work with Shakespeare because his texts are so well known or because the programme's originators see Shakespeare as 'universal'. When people are looking for drama therapy, they inevitably turn to Shakespeare—his reputation as 'best playwright' lends an automatic sense of prestige to almost any endeavour. Regardless of intent, such programmes tap into the potential benefits that many people may experience from participating in theatre more generally.

Surprisingly, both DE-CRUIT and the Hunter Heartbeat Method focus on iambic pentameter as a particularly 'therapeutic' form of verse. The popular mythology of iambic pentameter is wrapped up in the fame of William Shakespeare but also comes, in part, from its particular rhythm, which is often described as echoing the human heartbeat. The training of actors, and theatrical performance in general, include being attentive to both one's body and one's mind—and acting, at least what is generally considered good acting, usually requires some integration of the two. As Wiggins explains, Wolfert discovered that acting exercises helped him to manage the stress associated with PTSD: 'Actors must learn to control their breathing, and this led him [Wolfert] to see that he could regulate and ground himself through his performances.' Wolfert's sense that performing Shakespeare was particularly helpful for him because of the iambic pentameter verse was later confirmed by a study: as Wiggins explains, studies have shown that because 'the beat in Shakespeare's verse echoes the rhythm of the human heart', reciting iambic pentameter verse 'has been found helpful in reducing . . . heart rate variability' in people with PTSD. Wiggins also notes that breathing exercises used by actors were found to 'reduc[e] the stress response that is a key component of PTSD'. The Hunter Heartbeat Method, too, focuses on iambic pentameter verse as particularly significant, having the children start each session with what Hunter refers to as 'the Heartbeat Circle', in which children beat out the rhythm of 'hello' in time with their heartbeats (Hunter, *Shakespeare's Heartbeat*, 5).

However, the use of Shakespeare as therapy raises complex ideological problems. While participation in the arts may be pleasurable and provide a good creative outlet for many different people (able-bodied and disabled, neurotypical and neurodiverse alike), therapy and inclusion are not synonymous. In fact, the very concept of Shakespeare therapy *implies exclusion*. Espousing programmes that involve people with mental disabilities in the arts through therapy and rehabilitation may inadvertently imply that the only way that people with mental disabilities can be involved in the arts is through therapy and rehabilitation (and both practices are fundamentally designed to change the person with a disability). Assuming that the only way to engage particular disability communities in the arts is through art therapy is insulting and demeaning. It suggests that the attempt to offer cure or rehabilitation is the only way that able-bodied and neurotypical people can interact with people with disabilities. It may also inadvertently suggest that the arts belong to able-bodied and neurotypical people, who must give or bring the arts to people with disabilities. In fact, writers and artists with disabilities all too often encounter a prejudice that sees their work as therapy: reducing the work of artists with disabilities to the status of therapy is patronizing and devalues their art. Although DE-CRUIT works outside of the medical model of disability in many fruitful ways, the concept of theatre therapy originates in the medical model.

Autistic Culture and Shakespeare Therapy: the Hunter Heartbeat Method

Cultural stereotypes about autistic spectrum disabilities collide with cultural expectations about performing Shakespeare. Shakespeare is about words and language (autistic people often struggle with communication). Shakespeare is about strong emotion (autistic people may struggle to identify emotion and to express it in socially sanctioned ways). Shakespeare is about play and playing (autistic people, for the most part, do not play in ways that neurotypical people recognize as 'play'). However, the reasons for this imagined tension between cultural stereotypes of autism and cultural conceptions of Shakespeare may be more deep-seated and disturbing than they initially appear. Harold Bloom has infamously and bombastically claimed that Shakespeare invented the human.[5] The growing field of disability studies shows that autistic people face dehumanizing stereotypes and cultural practices—that autistic people may be falsely regarded as not-human or less-than-human because of mental disability. Thus, multiple tropes converge to render the term 'autistic Shakespearian' an oxymoron. Under Bloom's schema, to claim to engage Shakespeare is to claim to be fully human: fully capable of communication, emotion, and play.[6]

These imagined cultural tensions between the autistic subject's impairments and the performance of Shakespeare seem to inform some of the rhetoric undergirding and theoretical principles guiding the Hunter Heartbeat Method. Kelly Hunter, of the Royal Shakespeare Company, invented the programme a little over twenty years ago to provide social-skills therapy for autistic children.[7] Using role-playing games built on plots, characters, and lines from *The Tempest* and *A Midsummer Night's Dream*, the programme engages a variety of ages and the full breadth of the autism spectrum (ranging from non-verbal elementary-school-aged children to verbal teenagers).[8] One of the programme's major goals is to improve the social and communication abilities of autistic youth, focusing on skills such as eye contact, body language, and 'basic play'.[9] Paired one-on-one with adult actors who guide them through various games, autistic children are taught to imitate the facial expressions, vocal inflection, and body language of neurotypical adults as they embody various Shakespearian characters.

There are multiple strengths to the HHM approach. The practitioners of the HHM are enjoined to act with compassion and empathy toward the autistic children with whom they work, and the programme may encourage its neurotypical practitioners to build relationships with autistics, thus increasing autism awareness.[10] The HHM also teaches neurotypical educators to assume the competence of autistic children—this is a key tenet in working effectively with people with mental disabilities, since disability discrimination all too often begins with the assumption of the disabled subject's incompetence.[11] Because some autistic people are hypersensitive to sound and touch, the HHM allows for adaptations in activities that engage those senses: unlike some other autism therapies, Hunter's method encourages a respectful understanding of autistic sensory sensitivities (Hunter, *Shakespeare's Heartbeat*, 191–2). Finally, there is some possibility for autistic collaboration in the construction of the games themselves: practitioners are instructed to 'ensure that an enthusiastic suggestion from a child is greeted with equal enthusiasm from yourself and that you always try out their ideas' (Hunter, *Shakespeare's Heartbeat*, 228).

But while the HHM has led to the development of new communication and social skills in some autistic children, the programme often employs rhetoric that casts the autistic subject as an incomplete human being waiting to be 'awakened' (read: civilized, humanized) by Shakespeare. Bringing Shakespeare to autistic children is a charitable impulse, but it also bears the impulse of the cultural colonizer. Charity, an ancient practice that has all too often proscribed the interaction between the able-bodied and the disabled, evokes the power of those who give (neurotypical adults), the vulnerability of those who receive (autistic children), and the cultural capital of that which is given (Shakespeare's language). Indeed, the HHM builds on larger cultural assumptions dictating that Shakespeare is a universal good, a panacea with the power to 'heal' and 'cure', thus translating Shakespeare's cultural capital into a symbol of the medical model's desire for a world without mental disability.

The HHM (like some other forms of Shakespeare-based therapy) functions on beliefs that Shakespeare's language encapsulates and expresses the human experience and, therefore, that familiarity with Shakespeare is necessary in order to be a fully developed and 'healthy' human. Indeed, DE-CRUIT and the Hunter Heartbeat Method are part of a growing phenomenon of therapy/charity Shakespeares that Ayanna Thompson has termed 'Shakespeare reform programs', that Michael Jenson describes as 'Service Shakespeare', and that Geoffrey Ridden calls 'Shakespeare as therapy': such programmes target a diverse collection of minority groups including prison inmates, 'at-risk' youth, people who experience homelessness, and people with Alzheimer's disease.[12] The belief that Shakespeare's plays celebrate something quintessentially human is widespread, and Shakespeare therapy programmes may gain prestige and power based on such claims. As Matt Kozusko has argued, 'Shakespeare for some time has served a secular need for sacralized texts . . . the words are agreed to have a particular power . . . first as a means of capturing something essential and timeless about an audience's lived reality, and second as a means of validating and guaranteeing the fundamental humanity of that audience.'[13] As Alan Sinfield has pointed out, the classroom frequently engenders the belief that 'the plays reveal universal "human" values and qualities'.[14] Ironically, the cherished belief that Shakespeare's words contain something essentially human leads to the belief that to understand and appreciate Shakespeare's text therefore validates one's status as human.[15] When it comes to engaging Shakespeare's text, 'the pupil is being persuaded to internalize success or failure with particular and relative cultural codes as an absolute judgement on her or his potential as a human being'.[16] Thus, Shakespeare becomes a matrix of social belonging, dictating, to some extent, who belongs to a particular 'human' society and who does not.[17] To lack Shakespeare is to be cast outside of the social circle (or, perhaps, to lack the proper attributes of humanity altogether). Because 'a healthy public is one that both requires and celebrates the identifying markers of the human condition in its constituent members', to create a healthy body politic it becomes necessary to ensure that all members of the body politic have access to the 'healthy' and 'wholesome' texts of Shakespeare.[18]

This line of thinking has dangerous potential, particularly as it relates to those users of Shakespeare who have disabilities. From this logic (Shakespeare expresses the human and is therefore needed by all humans to validate their humanity) springs the belief that Shakespeare's language may have the ability to restore humanity where it is perceived to be lacking—the belief that Shakespeare's language might have the ability to heal. Ableist agendas have long presented people with disabilities as less-than-people or not-human. Thus, that which may restore or enliven humanity in the dehumanized subject (Shakespeare) might be imagined to have the power to end disability (the power to heal or cure). A popular culture faith in Shakespeare's potential to provide psychological, social, and emotional healing is surprisingly common. Denise Albanese has examined 'the pedagogical imperative that has attached to Shakespeare in the twentieth century, which takes as its agenda that Shakespeare is . . . good and good *for* you, if only you will learn to take it in properly . . . such a stance is so naturalized as to go without acknowledgment'.[19] Ridden has argued that 'Shakespeare has become so prevalent and powerful . . . as a shorthand to signal high culture that his name and his works can be invoked as therapeutic . . . ', and Thompson has examined the 'belief that personal reform can be achieved through Shakespearean study and performance'.[20] Historically, the medical model has presented disability as an individual problem in need of treatment and rehabilitation. Combining the search for treatment with a need to restore a fundamentally missing human nature, Shakespeare therapy fuses the medical model's agenda that seeks to eliminate disability from society through treatment or cure with the belief that those with disabilities will not be restored to full humanity without treatment or cure. Via this schema, the medical model of disability appropriates Shakespeare's cultural capital. In using Shakespeare as a potential source of healing and treatment, some Shakespeare therapies exist in a complex matrix of ideologies in which Shakespeare's cultural currency is used to authorize the medical model of disability—a model that many disability rights activists have rejected as oppressive, dehumanizing, and fundamentally colonial in its impulses and orientation.

Such therapy programmes may also be based on beliefs that Shakespeare is universal and that therefore Shakespeare should be made accessible to all people (including people with mental disabilities). As Marjorie Garber has argued, Shakespeare is 'the fantasy of originary cultural wholeness, the last vestige of universalism'.[21] Indeed, Kelly Hunter explains her motives in establishing the Hunter Heartbeat programme as being founded on Shakespeare's universality: 'I was preoccupied with the notion that Shakespeare's plays have untapped powers, inaccessible to many people through traditional means of performance and I was deeply frustrated by the overused maxim that "Shakespeare is for everyone". I absolutely agreed in the universality of Shakespeare's plays but . . . For me it sounded lazy to just say Shakespeare belonged to the people—I wanted to test that out' (Hunter, *Shakespeare's Heartbeat*, 234). In Shakespeare therapy, the belief that Shakespeare is universal results in the impetus *to make him universal*. If 'Shakespeare is for everyone' and yet there are minority groups who seem to lack access to Shakespeare, a colonial impulse is inspired: those who have Shakespeare must find a way to bring Shakespeare to those who are perceived to be without him.[22] In the case of disability communities, the question of Shakespeare's accessibility therefore becomes key. If Shakespeare is universal, then Shakespearians are challenged to ensure that those with disabilities are able to have equal access to his work. Accessibility is a central tenet of the disability rights movement and is a desirable goal in a variety of contexts. In fact, one of the highly lauded goals of disability studies as a critical field is to achieve universal design: for everything (from built spaces to social structures) to be accessible to everyone (no matter what kind of body or mind they may have) all of the time.

As many disability scholars have noted, universal design is desirable in theory but an unachievable goal in reality: it is impossible to design an environment that will equally accommodate everyone's needs simultaneously (see Chapter 2). In a similar way, a project to make Shakespeare 'universal', 'accessible', and 'inclusive' must necessarily create a Shakespeare that meets the needs of many diverse groups; striving for a 'universal' Shakespeare is much like striving for universal design. The goal is unattainable: a version of Shakespeare that speaks to one audience may not communicate well with another, and no amount of translation, adaptation, or accessibility is likely to create a Shakespeare that communicates equally well with all audiences and all cultures in all circumstances. In light of the failure of both universal design and universal Shakespeare, some Shakespeare-based therapies ultimately adopt the opposite approach to making Shakespeare 'universal'. If Shakespeare cannot be made to meet the needs of a particular minority group, then the minority group must be changed (through therapy) to meet the majority groups' expectations of what Shakespeare should be: thus, such programmes try to change the disabled subject in order to meet the needs of a rigidly neurotypical conception of Shakespeare. (True accessibility would require neurotypical Shakespearians to change conceptions of what Shakespeare is and how it should be performed in order to meet the needs of people with mental disabilities.) What begins as an impulse to bring Shakespeare to those with mental disabilities ultimately becomes the impetus to eliminate (to cure or treat) mental disabilities. Ironically, the endeavour to make Shakespeare accessible, universal, and inclusive has led to the effort to eliminate disabled diversity through the (presumably homogenizing) power of Shakespeare's text. The narratives we tell about Shakespeare being 'good for us' have both persuasive and dangerous cultural power: if observers are expecting a certain narrative (the narrative of Shakespeare being able to psychologically, emotionally, and socially heal the disabled, oppressed, and/or outcast), then users of Shakespeare may be overlooking other narratives (such as the need for social change).[23] In this way, Shakespeare's assumed complicity in and affirmation of the medical model of disability may draw attention away from the disability rights' movement and its call for social equality for people with mental disabilities.

What if Shakespeare is the cure? Passing and Performing Neurotypical

Indeed, the HHM (vis-à-vis Shakespeare as cure) is firmly wedded to the medical model of disability: in overlooking the neurodiversity paradigm, the programme prioritizes treatment for autism over the need for social acceptance for autistic people. Traditionally, the medical model has focused on 'treatment' and 'cure' for people on the spectrum. However, the neurodiversity movement that has grown within the autism community works in tandem with the larger disability rights movement to oppose the medical model. Recognizing autistic behaviour as a difference rather than a deficit, the neurodiversity movement argues that such mental differences are a normal part of human diversity. Espousing neurodiversity, members of the disability rights movement recognize autistic people as a cultural minority group who form a community with shared experiences and values. Autistic activists and self-advocates point out that some autistic traits (memory skills, single-minded focus, honesty) can also be strengths. Autistic culture commonly celebrates autistic characteristics that psychologists consider to be deficits as sources of fulfilment and joy. For example, people on the autism spectrum often have 'special interests' (interests that are unusual in subject or depth) and engage in self-stimulatory behaviours (commonly known as 'stimming') such as pacing, rocking, and hand-flapping. Many autistic adults consider such characteristics to be a central part of self-identity; some people on the spectrum find special interests to be deeply fulfilling and enjoy engaging in stimming. Rather than seeking a cure or a treatment for autism, the neurodiversity movement works for disability accommodations and social acceptance for autistic people. In other words, instead of trying to change the disabled child, the neurodiversity movement seeks to change societal attitudes toward disability. However, the practitioners of the HHM frequently seem out of touch with the concerns of the neurodiversity movement and of the autistic community, addressing autism in terms that evoke the medical model's focus on deficit, cure, and treatment.

Despite the HHM's emphasis on providing a treatment for autism, it seems unlikely that Shakespeare is the 'cure' for neurodiversity and that children's neurology is being fundamentally changed by this ten-week programme: it is more likely that the programme is teaching autistic children the skills needed to pass as neurotypical. People with disabilities passing as non-disabled has a long history, and a great deal of critical ink has been spilt on the subject of 'passing' in the field of disability studies. As Ellen Samuels explains, 'Like racial, gender, and queer passing, the option of passing as nondisabled provides both a certain level of privilege and a profound sense of misrecognition and internal dissonance.'[24] Although those who pass as non-disabled may 'avoid the perceived stigma attached to a disabled identity', passing has significant costs: 'if... disabled people pursue normalization too much, they risk denying limitations and pain for the comfort of others and may edge into the self-betrayal associated with passing.'[25] The consensus among autistic adults is that passing for neurotypical is often exhausting: spending long hours attempting to imitate neurotypical body language, dealing with environments that aggravate sensory sensitivities, and ignoring the need to stim can all cause frustration, fatigue, and even physical pain. Indeed, passing can also have a lasting psychological toll, since it may involve the public denial of identity (a decision not to be 'out' as autistic). In spite of the potential problems with passing, the HHM's focus on 'treating' autism may be promoting passing skills for autistic children rather than providing a fundamental change in neurology.

The HHM's rhetoric is clearly in line with the medical model: the programme's language sidesteps the issue of autistic identity and unquestioningly forwards passing as a desirable goal for people with disabilities. A new study from the Ohio State University shows that the students involved in the programme are changing their social skills: 'An initial pilot study with 14 students with ASD [autistic spectrum disorder] yielded data indicating positive changes in the students' interpersonal skills, pragmatic language, and overall adaptive behavior after a ten-week intervention.'[26] In the analysis of these results, the 'deficit-based' assumptions of the Shakespeare-based therapy are clear: 'Overall, the Heartbeat Method shows promise regarding the improvement of core deficits associated with autism spectrum disorder....'[27] The HHM is a 'minimal treatment dose' which only requires a 'once-weekly intervention'.[28] Although current medical consensus acknowledges that there is no 'cure' for autism, Shakespeare is being considered as a possible 'treatment', a way for society to change the social development of the autistic child: 'the research team is assessing the ability of these games to affect [*sic*] significant and long-term change to the core features of autism.'[29] In such statements, it is accepted without question that changing the 'core features of autism' is a desirable goal and that naturally everyone (including autistic people) should seek that goal. However, the medical model's focus on changing the individual means that people may ignore the need for larger social change—overlooking the role that society plays in disadvantaging those with cognitive differences.

Furthermore, the programme's Shakespeare-based games are teaching skills that autistic children can use to pass as neurotypical, thus transforming Shakespeare into a tool that 'normalizes' the autistic subject; Shakespeare's text authorizes the HHM, lending cultural authority to the imperative to pass. Key games in the HHM focus on eliminating autistic body language and replacing it with neurotypical body language. For example, the 'lovers' magic trance' is a role-playing game loosely based on *The Tempest* in which Ariel guides Ferdinand to Miranda. Hunter describes the 'lovers' magic trance' as 'a key game providing the opportunity for the children to explore a smooth, flowing physical language, counteracting the awkward stiffness that they so often experience' (Hunter, *Shakespeare's Heartbeat*, 165). This activity teaches children to mask autistic body language and to mimic neurotypical body movements. Like many of the games in the HHM, the game requires extensive eye focus and eye contact (Ferdinand and Miranda must maintain eye contact at the end of the sequence) as well as the ability to imitate neurotypical body language (the child imitates her neurotypical partner's movements as Ariel guides Ferdinand). In other words, the game teaches children how to 'look' neurotypical and rewards them for changing autistic body language. In fact, autistic movements only look 'awkward' and 'stiff' from a neurotypical perspective (stimming, based on the aesthetic pleasure of repetition and sensory appeals, can be seen as beautiful). Autistic body language is only disabling when people discriminate against those who display such body language. Clearly, there is a philosophical and ethical tension in questions of autistic passing. On the one hand, teaching autistic children to pass may teach them invaluable life skills that will help them to function in a world of neurotypical social expectations. On the other hand, teaching autistic children to pass may not help to increase social acceptance for autistic identity and expression. In short, games like the 'lovers' magic trance' may teach children to hide autistic identity: the HHM, in its efforts to 'cure' autism, may simply forward passing for people with disabilities.

Even assuming that the HHM causes a fundamental change in neurology, one would have to question whether changing the brain function of an autistic child is ethically acceptable. Although brain scan technology has not yet been used to verify the results of the HHM, other drama therapy programmes have shown changes in brain activity based on such scans:

> [R]esearch from Vanderbilt University showed improved communication and social skills and better memory for faces in children with ASD who had participated in a 10-week, 40-hour drama therapy program. In that study, scientists used brain-imaging technology to look at brain-frequency levels in the children who had completed the program as one part of the research. They found that the kids who had been in the program had brain frequency levels that were more similar to children without autism.[30]

If autistic children grow into autistic adults (as they inevitably do) and many autistic adults regard autism as central to their identity, is it morally right to change how the brains of autistic people work? Do fundamental changes to a person's brain change who that person is? The article cited above offers a photo of autistic children engaged in the HHM. Under the photo is the caption, 'The bard can fix anything'.[31] Clearly, the implication is that autistic people need to be 'fixed' and that Shakespeare can be used to fix them. The caption implicitly says that autistic people are broken.

'This island's mine': Resisting the Colonization of Autistic Culture

One of the founding principles of the disability rights movement is the concept of disability as a source of identity and community: however, the rhetoric of the HHM prioritizes treatment over identity and/or community. Although autistics also participate in face-to-face gatherings like the annual Autreat, much of autistic culture is created and sustained via the internet: online interaction allows autistics to come together while avoiding the pitfalls of face-to-face socialization, the challenges of verbal vocalization, and the difficulties of unwelcoming sensory environments. In other words, the internet offers the ideal realm for autistic socialization, with a resultant explosion of online autistic communities (such as Wrong Planet) and advocacy organizations (such as the Autistic Self Advocacy Network). Autistic blogging has reached the level of art form, with a large number of influential autistic activists gathering large followings on neurodiversity blogs. Over time, the autistic community has developed a unique culture of its own: 'Within a medical model, autism is constructed by professionals—psychiatrists, psychologists, educators—in their articles, books, and clinical practices. Within a social model, autism is constructed by autistic people themselves through the culture they produce (including writing, art, and music), and its shared features give it cohesion and a distinctive identity.'[32] As autistic activist Jim Sinclair explains,

> We have certain shared values in affirming the validity of our way of being. We have many common experiences both with the experience of autism itself, and with being autistic in a world of neurotypicals. We have a history of significant events experienced by our community. We have a dynamic, constantly-evolving set of customs and rules growing out of our shared experiences and our common needs. We have certain terms, expressions, and in-jokes that are distinct to our community.[33]

One unique element of autistic culture is the celebration of stimming, an activity which is, in many ways, the autistic equivalent of neurotypical play. As autistic activist Julia Bascom explains the pleasures of stimming,

> flapping your hands *just so* amplifies everything you feel and thrusts it up into the air . . . It takes a million different forms. A boy pacing by himself, flapping and humming and laughing. An 'interest' or obsession that is 'age appropriate'—or maybe one that is not. A shake of the fingers in front of the eyes, a monologue, an echolaliated phrase. All of these things autistic people are supposed to be ashamed of and stop doing? *They are how we communicate our joy.*[34]

Indeed, some autistic activists have argued that stimming, as a form of self-expression, is a uniquely autistic language.[35] That autistic children do not usually engage in activities that neurotypical people consider to be play (for example, hobbies, games, pretend play) has been frequently noted.[36] That autistics might have their own ways to play (such as stimming) has been frequently overlooked.

In fact, one of the HHM's primary objectives is to teach autistic children how to 'play'; this objective seems to be based on our culture's commonly held misconception that autistic people have no prior existing culture (and thus, forms of play) of their own. It is true that autistic children's refusal to play in socially sanctioned ways is often regarded as a symptom of pathology; the autistic child may demonstrate a 'lack of interest in toys, or plays with them in an unusual way (e.g., lining up, spinning, opening/closing parts rather than playing with the toy as a whole)', and psychologists frequently cite a lack of 'pretend play' as a 'developmental deficit' in autistic people.[37] (Notice, however, that the 'unusual' ways to play listed in the above example—lining up, spinning, opening/closing—are all examples of stimming. This tactile manipulation of objects, which actively engages the autistic imagination, is interpreted by the neurotypical observer as a lack of ability to be 'creative'.) Anne McGuire describes 'the ways in which disabled children's play has been transformed by the field of developmental psychology as an instrument of surveillance, measurement, and evaluation'.[38] This cultural 'policing' of play suggests the level of scrutiny (and potential censure) to which autistic children may be subject. Autistic stimming and neurotypical play are somewhat analogous: stimming and pretend play are both pleasurable ways of spending leisure time; stimming, like pretend play, can actively evoke engagement with imagination.

The HHM seems to be a part of the larger cultural discourse that seeks to police and limit autistic play and to encourage neurotypical play in its place. According to Hunter, the therapy's 'ultimate aim no matter where the children are on the spectrum is for them to experience what a game *feels* like' (Hunter, *Shakespeare's Heartbeat*, 24). Because play as a concept is neither ahistorical nor acultural, what is primarily being taught through the HHM is what play feels like and is defined as for and by neurotypical people. This strong emphasis on teaching neurotypical play appears throughout Kelly Hunter's book *Shakespeare's Heartbeat*, which serves as the 'treatment manual' for the HHM. Hunter encourages practitioners to 'Never give up on the child's ability to play' and wonders about the implications of researching play as a measurable result of the programme: 'It will be interesting to see how important the art of playfulness is within the findings of the research and whether in fact playfulness is deemed measurable at all. I've tried to convey the significance of playfulness within the games . . .' (Hunter, *Shakespeare's Heartbeat*, 225; 238). In *Shakespeare's Heartbeat*, Hunter presents playfulness as central to the human experience. Since our culture often conceives of autistic children as children who fundamentally lack the ability to play, it is all too often believed that these children are therefore incapable of basic human attributes. Hunter sees the therapy as giving autistic children an opportunity that all children should have but that autistic children lack: 'all children with autism are indeed children and all children deserve the chance to play' (Hunter, *Shakespeare's Heartbeat*, 239). This desire to teach play is based on a colonialist impulse—the idea is that neurotypical educators know how to play and that they can teach autistic children how to resemble them. Specifically, Shakespeare is the medium through which the HHM teaches neurotypical conceptions of play. Children are encouraged to speak a neurotypical language, to move through the world in neurotypical ways, to engage in neurotypical play—to adopt the culture of the neurotypical colonizer, who is charitably bringing Shakespeare (read: humanity) to autistics.

It is symbolically appropriate that one of the two plays used in the HHM is *The Tempest*, a play with a celebrated history of postcolonial performances and interpretations: Shakespeare's text (presented in the HHM in a series of games that focus on teaching language, imperialist impulses, and cultural power dynamics) comes to symbolize the programme's colonization of the autistic subject. In *The Tempest* games, the slaves of the imperialist Prospero are central roles for the autistic children to focus on and learn to perform: 'These first games use Caliban as a focus for the children', and '*The Tempest* games focus also on themes of liberty and imprisonment using the characters of Caliban and Ariel to provide a deeper means for the children to express themselves' (Hunter, *Shakespeare's Heartbeat*, 121; 9). The game of 'Teaching Caliban to speak' has a multilayered symbolic resonance in this context, since some of the autistic children who engage in the HHM are nonverbal (some may communicate by signing or typing but not by speaking). In this game, 'Caliban is gabbling, making noise with no language. He is moving around the circle on all fours, making a never-ending clamorous babble' (Hunter, *Shakespeare's Heartbeat*, 139). Miranda says, 'My name is Miranda. Your name is Caliban', in an effort to get Caliban to speak his name (Hunter, *Shakespeare's Heartbeat*, 139). The choice to engage children with a communication disability in a game about learning to speak is already symbolically laden, as playing the game may evoke the frustration that neurotypicals experience in attempting to communicate with autistics (and that autistics experience in attempting to communicate with neurotypicals). Furthermore, because verbal stimming is common among autistic children, practitioners may find it difficult to convince the child performing the role of Caliban to stop stimming and to switch over to neurotypical pretend play. As Hunter explains, 'A few children enjoy the babbling so much that they willfully refuse to stop, and if after a few attempts they can't move on from the babbling, abandon the game' (Hunter, *Shakespeare's Heartbeat*, 142). In Shakespeare's play, Miranda is unable to recognize that Caliban may have a prior language and culture of his own—although it is possible that what she calls 'gabble' is the language of his mother, Sycorax (*The Tempest*, 1.2.355–9). The HHM seems to function on the premise that autistic people have no prior language or culture that is unique to the autistic community. Just as Shakespeare's Miranda does not recognize Caliban's 'gabble' as a possible foreign tongue, the HHM does not recognise stimming as a possible mode of play and expression. Even more significantly, the passage alluded to from *The Tempest* may draw the attention of some participants and viewers to the colonial impulses underlying developmental psychology, the modern special education classroom, and the HHM itself.

Although Shakespeare's text is not directly used in this particular game, Miranda's words from *The Tempest* may uncomfortably haunt the image of the neurotypical adult teaching the autistic child to speak. This is especially true when the autistic child plays Caliban and the neurotypical practitioner of the HHM plays Miranda:

> I pitied thee,
> Took pains to make thee speak, taught thee each hour
> One thing or other. When thou didst not, savage,
> Know thine own meaning, but wouldst gabble like

> A thing most brutish, I endowed thy purposes
> With words that made them known.
>
> (1.2.355–60)

In this passage, not only is Miranda positioned as the able-bodied subject that gives magnanimously (and charitably) but Caliban is positioned as both ungrateful and unknowing. Although Shakespeare's textual Caliban is probably more likely to be interpreted as racially Other (rather than disabled), the colonial impulse that polices the racialized body is bound up in the same cultural logic that attempts to treat and cure the disabled body.[39] As McGuire argues, there is a connection between modern developmental psychology (the branch of the medical model that diagnoses and treats autism) and the history of colonialism:

> The developmental perspective dominated (and continues to dominate) colonial rule, particularly through ideologies spawned by evolutionism. Colonial dominance was/is maintained through the surveillance and policing of all bodies, the sharpening of the boundaries separating normal from abnormal development and the recognition that departures and deviations from 'normal' (and, thus, always and already white, male, able-bodied, heterosexual, and middle-classed) development represented somatic *pathologies*. Under colonial logic, people of color and indigenous people, queer, disabled and poor people . . . became conceptually linked though their purported pathological deviance from the esteemed status of 'fully' developed human. The biomedical gaze that watches for and recognizes difference as pathology simultaneously inaugurates the necessity for biomedical/pedagogical interventions that aim to restore not simply health but also civility.[40]

In the colonial perspective, all Othered bodies are pathologized bodies that fail to reach 'the esteemed status of "fully" developed human'. And such less-than-human creatures create a demand for 'biomedical/pedagogical intervention'—a need that both Shakespeare's Miranda and the HHM try to meet.

Miranda's effort to teach Caliban to speak stems from a charitable impulse ('I pitied thee'). Originally funded by charitable organizations, the HHM relies on the long-standing charity schema that has determined power structures between the able-bodied and the disabled for hundreds of years (Hunter, *Shakespeare's Heartbeat,* 235). Miranda gives Caliban language. The HHM gives autistic children Shakespeare. The charity system highlights the superior social position of those who give (neurotypicals) and the dispossessed position of those who receive (autistics). It also draws attention to the cultural power of that which is given through such acts of charity. Hunter's rhetoric describes autistic people as though they were 'asleep', unaware of their own lives and experiences: 'This lies at the heart of the work, the fundamental aim of which is to use Shakespeare as a means of waking the children up to their own lives' (Hunter, *Shakespeare's Heartbeat*, 155). In *Shakespeare's Heartbeat*, Shakespeare is imagined as a life-giving force (the heartbeat) that will make autistic people fully alive—and fully human. In short, *The Tempest* games of the HHM subtly suggest the imperialist impulse at work between the neurotypical colonizer and the colonized autistic child.

Conclusion: Autistic Ways to Play

My students think that I read Shakespeare beautifully. (I know, because they often say so, with obvious delight and wonder, asking how they can learn to read it as well as I do.) Shakespeare's easy numbers flow from my lips readily and naturally, with the facility of long familiarity. I also know that, like all of the words that I speak, Shakespeare's lines bear the monotone timbre born of autism, that I speak Shakespeare's words with almost no outwardly discernible intonation or emotional expression. Given my students' responses, I am not convinced that this mode of speaking Shakespeare is inherently flawed—indeed, it could be seen as uniquely beautiful, an authentically autistic appropriation of Shakespeare's language. In our culture, disability is so often thought of as a deficit that very little thought is given to the possibility that disability might create art or act creatively. But my teaching of Shakespeare clearly springs from mental disability, from a distinctively autistic experience of the world. And my teaching is both joyful and playful (just not in ways that are readily translatable to neurotypical definitions of 'joy' and 'play'). The HHM seems, on some fundamental levels, to assume that Shakespeare and disability are separate worlds—and that if we could somehow unite these worlds, it would be a powerful and 'healing' unity. I can only hope that, as we continue to explore and experiment with the HHM, we will not foreclose the possibility of explicitly autistic Shakespeares—that we will not shut down or invalidate autistic notions of what it means to play.

4

Neurodiverse Shakespeares

Mental Disability in Still Dreaming

A conflict between the young and the old is an ancient device of stage comedy. Rarely can two different generations perfectly understand each other: the passage of time ensures that they come from slightly different cultures (often the older and younger version of the same culture) and that they speak slightly different languages (often the older and younger version of the same language). The changes wrought by the passage of time mean that the younger generation and the older one often have different bodies of knowledge and different life goals. Hank Rogerson and Jilann Spitzmiller's *Still Dreaming* is a documentary that examines the creation of an unusual performance: two directors go into an assisted living facility and lead the residents in staging a production of *A Midsummer Night's Dream*. As the young directors encourage the elderly actors to engage with Shakespeare's comedy, invoking the age-old formula of the younger generation versus the older one, the expected comedic conflicts occur. Indeed, this dynamic replicates the outline of Shakespeare's play, in which the young lovers must escape the oppressive dictates of marriage that have been forced upon them by the father's generation. The young characters flee their elders, escaping into the magical forest, and their belief in love is eventually validated and made triumphant by the magic they find there. However, the two young directors in *Still Dreaming* are also presented as able-bodied and neurotypical, while the elderly residents of the assisted living facility have various disabilities. Rogerson and Spitzmiller's film presents the clash of cultures that may arise not only when the younger generation encounters the

Shakespeare and Disability Studies. Sonya Freeman Loftis, Oxford University Press (2021).
 DOI: 10.1093/oso/9780198864530.003.0005

older one but also when the able-bodied encounter the disabled and the neurotypical encounter the neurodiverse. Although the film comedically depicts the symbolic triumph of youth over age and celebrates the triumph of life over death, it does not espouse popular culture's stereotypical prioritizing of able-bodiedness and neurotypicality over disability. The film begins by suggesting an overcoming narrative that lauds the power of Shakespeare. However, *Still Dreaming* ultimately concludes that those who are able-bodied and neurotypical can learn to embrace disability culture and neurodiverse ways of understanding relationships, accessibility, sensory perceptions, and time, exploring theatre as the symbolic medium through which this union of the neurotypical and the neurodiverse takes place.

Interdependency, Accessibility, and Crip Time in *Still Dreaming*

From the beginning, *Still Dreaming*'s narrative toys with stereotypical expectations regarding disability and common clichés regarding narratives of Shakespearian performance. The two directors of the film's play-within-the-film, Ben Steinfeld and Noah Brody, undertake their task—preparing a group of retired actors to perform *A Midsummer Night's Dream*—with obvious uncertainty and scepticism. The introductory words that appear on the dark screen at the beginning of the film reinforce both Steinfeld's and Brody's youthfulness as well as the perceived difficulty of their task: 'The staff has recently offered a challenge to the residents to emerge from retirement to put on a Shakespeare play. Two acclaimed (up-and-coming) Shakespearean directors have been hired out of New York City to guide the process. For the next six weeks, the residents will get the chance to work at a professional level again'.[1] Steinfeld and Brody are parenthetically described as 'up-and-coming', thus highlighting their relative youth and inexperience, while their task is labelled a 'challenge'. As they enter the assisted living facility, Steinfeld says, 'Alright. What the hell do we do now?', only for Brody to respond, 'Now what? I have no idea'. Because the purpose of an assisted living facility is to help those who may be unable to live independently, ageist and ableist assumptions might lead some to conclude that those who are unable to live 'independently' would also not be ready for the rigours of putting on a Shakespeare play. However, disability studies as a critical field has long questioned ideologies of independence, pointing out that most people are interdependent and that very few people actually live independently.[2] (How many people grow their own food, make their own clothes, and otherwise eschew any interaction with other humans?) In reality, most humans depend on other humans to help them meet some of their daily needs. As Lennard J. Davis explains it, 'dependence is the reality, and independence grandiose thinking'.[3] Thus, disability studies scholars tend to espouse the notion of 'interdependence' rather than independence, pointing out that what counts as 'independence' is an ideological construct. The prioritizing and valorizing of imagined independence means that those who are seen as 'dependent' are often thought of as weak or needy. All the elderly residents of the assisted living facility are living interdependently, and most also have significant impairments; this leaves the staff of the facility, the able-bodied directors, and some of the residents themselves wondering whether these particular actors will be able to perform a Shakespeare play.

Indeed, the film follows many of the formulaic tropes familiar to stories about disability that are laid out in Chapter 1: *Still Dreaming* asks questions about disability when the answers are already known and uses this method to set the film up for a heroic-overcomer narrative. The performance takes place at the Lillian Booth Actors' Home, an assisted living facility specifically designed for retired actors and performers. Thus, the question the staff and directors worry over at the beginning of the film ('will the residents be able to put on a play?') has already been answered in the very name of the facility itself: the residents are professional actors, and although they have acquired impairments and are retired from the stage, this does not necessarily mean that they will no longer be able to perform a Shakespeare play. It is no particular surprise to find that a group of actors with disabilities, given the right accommodations, can, in fact, act. A scene early in the film, in which a receptionist answers questions about the show in response to curious queries on the phone, may remind viewers of this reality: 'Actors Fund. Yeah, I don't know the exact date. They are doing *A Midsummer Night's Dream*. Most of the residents *are* residents. Yeah... call again and I'll get the exact date.' Are the residents with disabilities in fact residents at the assisted living facility and are they putting on a play? Yes, they are. Although the questions the film poses are often phrased as 'what are the residents with disabilities able to do?', it seems clear that people are more often wondering, 'what kinds of accommodations will the residents need?' As the facility's director explains, 'There's some trepidation, some nervousness—you know some of those questions that we've had internally amongst staff is "What can we really expect out of the residents?" And to have them engage every day for six weeks is going to be a lot for them.' Thus, the narrative begins by questioning the ability of the residents with disabilities and presents putting on a play as a challenge that the film's narrative will follow them in 'overcoming'.

Indeed, the hesitant uncertainty of the young directors in approaching the production (and in trying to decide what kinds of accommodations are needed and how those accommodations will change the performance of the play) makes the more experienced actors wary in their early interactions with them; thus, the comedic battle for power between the two generations begins in the opening scenes of the film. As Steinfeld says at their first rehearsal, 'I'm just really thrilled that Noah [Brody] and I get to learn from all of you, from your experiences and your artistry, and from your unique points of view about this play. And you know, we don't know, we have no idea, what the show will be. We will be asking ourselves the question: What does it mean to do *A Midsummer Night's Dream* here with you?' The older actors look dubious and amused by the young directors' uncertainty. In fact, the residents begin to interrogate the two directors almost immediately: 'Do you have a basic idea of what is going to hold it all together?' and 'You're not going to do the whole play are you?' However, the directors are open to the needs of the residents and to being flexible, and respond by asking questions like 'What does success mean for us?', 'What does a production mean for us?', and 'What are your hopes and desires for this process and this production?' In this way, the directors show that they will be responsive to the needs of the residents and that they want the participants to define the parameters of the show. Yet the young directors leave the first rehearsal feeling uncertain, questioning whether the mobility impairments of the actors will make it difficult to stage a full production: 'I didn't get the sense that anyone was too comfortable walking around—at all. Now I don't know what—are we going to do a complete version of this play at all?' Some of the actors use wheelchairs or canes, and many of them experience fatigue. It is surprising that the directors initially wonder whether mobility impairments will be a major challenge to the show, since many of the difficulties that later emerge relate to mental disability rather than to physical impairment.

In addition to highlighting some potential conflicts between the directors and the actors, the early rehearsals also raise questions regarding artistic integrity and disability accommodation, thus showing a clash between mainstream able-bodied expectations of art and the expectations of disability culture. Although many of the residents have acquired impairments, some of them still hold strongly to an able-bodied/neurotypical conception of what theatre, and Shakespeare, should be. In particular, the elderly actors, many of whom have memory impairments, question whether they can, or should, attempt to memorize the play text, a conflict that almost immediately leads to a loud argument:

> HAROLD CHERRY: Are we memorizing these? Because I'm just asking. Because some people will have difficulty.
>
> DIMO CONDOS: What kind of a question is that? Are you talking about some people or are you talking about yourself?
>
> HAROLD CHERRY: Whatever.
>
> DIMO CONDOS: You want to play Bottom without memorizing it?
>
> HAROLD CHERRY: Of course, I'm going to memorize it.
>
> DIMO CONDOS: Then why do you ask: 'Do I have to memorize?' What the hell kind of acting is that? Of course, you have to memorize!
>
> HAROLD CHERRY: Okay!
>
> BRODY: We know you can act without having memorized your lines because we've seen it now for over a week... it is far premature to assume that memorization is what is needed to get acting going...
>
> STEINFELD: We hope that you will memorize if you want to memorize. Not being memorized is not going to be a stumbling block or a problem in this production.

Among the participants, Aideen O'Kelly and Dimo Condos feel strongly that memorization of Shakespeare's text should be required, implying in various ways that the residents are not able to do 'real' acting if they are not able to memorize. Initially, both O'Kelly and Condos are not willing to let their need for accommodations alter their vision of what 'performing Shakespeare' should mean. The false fear that disability accommodations will somehow damage artistic merit or academic integrity is common. However, the lively, entertaining, and funny production of *A Midsummer Night's Dream* that closes the film is only one piece of evidence representing the many ways in which such claims are untrue. It is obviously possible to do a compelling performance of Shakespeare's work with script in hand, and for many of the residents with memory impairments this is the only kind of performance that can include them. However, even from the first rehearsal the directors feel a need to defend their production as 'real Shakespeare': 'We will have a real show, and we will have a real script'. The directors' insistence that this is *real art* and *real theatre* attempts to defend the play from those residents who believe that there is only one standard—an able-bodied and neurotypical one—for what the performance of Shakespeare can and should be.

This tension between the need for disability accommodations and mainstream able-bodied cultural expectations of art and performance is further exemplified in both O'Kelly's current experiences and her past history. Ironically, even though O'Kelly originally argued that memorization is necessary for 'real' acting, she has such a difficult time memorizing her lines that she ultimately ends up withdrawing from the production. While O'Kelly claims that she bows out of the show due to concerns about her health, various scenes suggest that her real reason for withdrawing is that the performance is not able to fully accommodate her. O'Kelly has an acquired visual impairment, which was one of the primary reasons for her retirement from the stage. As she explains, 'The trouble is I can't see to read at all no matter what. I can't use a script the way that some people do. That's why I had to give up acting actually. It was forced retirement. I used to think I was one of those people who want to die with their boots on. But this is a great place to be, considering . . . I can't be at it, as some people say'. The final form that the performance of *A Midsummer Night's Dream* takes allows for a variety of disability accommodations for the actors. In the end, no one memorizes his or her part completely, and the entire cast ends up doing a performance with script in hand. Those with fatigue rest in chairs at the side of the performance space when they are offstage. Charlotte Fairchild, whom the film describes as having Alzheimer's disease, is accompanied by her one-on-one aid (who acts as a fairy attending Fairchild's Puck). Although O'Kelly attempts to memorize her lines by listening to them on tape, she finds that she cannot remember them. While the format of the final show is otherwise very flexible, it is disappointing when the directors do not find a way to accommodate O'Kelly, who initially had been very enthusiastic about her involvement in the performance.

Throughout the film, the young directors attempt to use Shakespeare's text to draw connections between able-bodied experiences and the lived experience of disability. For example, the theme of questioning the perception of the senses comes up repeatedly as the directors and actors work together to analyse the text of *A Midsummer Night's Dream*. Brody glosses the line, 'Methinks I see these things with parted eye, / When everything seems double' (4.1.188–9), as meaning, 'Are you seeing what I'm seeing?' This commentary on vision speaks to O'Kelly's experience of visual impairment: 'You said literally seeing double? . . . Well I do because my eyesight is double, and it floats around . . . .' Steinfeld agrees with her: 'I think they [in the play] are saying it is literally that thing you are describing—a medical thing. But it is also perspective.' Of course, one of the lessons of disability studies is that sometimes 'medical things' do, in fact, shape and inform our sensory perceptions and therefore our perspectives. In another scene, Steinfeld explains that 'Bottom can't trust his senses here. Which I would imagine is incredibly frightening, if you have an experience where you actually can't trust fully what you are seeing or be sure of what you are hearing.' The distorted lens of the camera during this scene renders the sight of the rehearsal room blurry, ensuring that viewers cannot trust their sight of the scene. As the director finishes speaking, the camera focuses in on O'Kelly, whose acting career ended when accommodations were not provided for her visual impairment. In this way, the film presents the theme of what is seen, and not seen, in *A Midsummer Night's Dream* as a parallel to O'Kelly's sense of 'double eyesight'.

In other scenes, the neurotypical directors try to interpret Shakespeare's text in ways that may relate to neurodiverse experiences regarding sensory perceptions. As they are cutting the text, Brody notes that 'the themes that have come up that I think have been really useful for anchoring the production are perspective: the difference between something that happened and something that might have happened or something that you dreamed and something that you experienced and so it's just a reminder that any experience that you have is your truth.' Neurodiversity can create a variety of sensory perceptions and experiences that may be subjective, and some neurodiverse sensory perceptions are unique to the individual who has them. Hallucinations and delusions certainly change sensory perceptions and experiences. However, even autistic sensory issues can cause one to question a sense of objective shared reality. If an autistic person and a neurotypical person are standing in the same space and the autistic person perceives the space to be extremely noisy but the neurotypical person perceives the space to be only a little noisy, which of them is right? While Brody's commentary on the play, which remarks that 'any experience that you have is your truth', seems to affirm a neurodiverse perspective in which almost all perceptions are, on some level, subjective, the two directors have a hard time living out that kind of philosophy as they work with the residents at the assisted living facility.

The film clearly draws a parallel between the disorienting events that take place in the enchanted forest of *A Midsummer Night's Dream* and the sensory perceptions of the neurodiverse actors. When the directors describe the plot of the play to the residents, some of the actors are confused. Steinfeld agrees that the plot is confusing and goes on to note that the experience of being lost in the woods under a magic spell would probably be pretty disorienting as well: 'There's a lot more darkness and confusion that accompanies all of this stuff which makes it funny for us. But for the people who are experiencing it—it is kind of terrifying sometimes.' This analysis of the play clearly parallels Gloria Albee's later explanation about her experience of memory impairment: 'My short term memory is like . . . you know . . . ask me what I did when I was eight years old and I can tell you, but I can't tell you what I did two seconds ago. And it's very frustrating and a little unnerving.' In this way, the film draws a parallel between the confusion of the characters who are lost in the woods and Albee's experience of memory impairment.

However, Steinfeld soon discovers difficulties in his attempts to bring neurotypical and neurodiverse expectations together: agreeing on a shared perception of reality and achieving clear communication between neurodiverse and neurotypical people both come to the forefront as potential challenges. When Albee tells Steinfeld that she is leaving the Actors' Home to move across the country, he is distraught, since she is one of the best actors in the show. Albee tells Steinfeld that he will have to find someone else to play her part, and he jokingly responds, 'Like in the play, I can't tell right now if this is happening or if it's some kind of nightmare. No, I'm just teasing you. I'm going to talk to Yalile [Alzate] about it tomorrow, and I'm just going to be in denial about everything you just told me.' However, when Steinfeld speaks with Yalile Alzate, director of recreation at the Lillian Booth Actors' Home, he is surprised by what he discovers:

> ALZATE: She's not moving. That's only imagination. She thinks she is. And this is reflective of her past life. She always moved a lot before she came to the Actors' Home, so she is always saying 'I'm moving.' It's not happening. She's here.
>
> STEINFELD: Well, that's good news for us. But it's bad news for her that she thinks she is because I don't want her to be disappointed.
>
> ALZATE: Don't worry. She's going to go to bed today, and tomorrow she'll start over. Maybe she's moving or maybe it will be something else. But it's okay.
>
> STEINFELD: How do you do this every day?
>
> ALZATE [LAUGHING]: I've been doing it for so many years, so I'm just used to it.
>
> STEINFELD: Alright. Well—I admire you a lot.

The viewer may be as surprised as Steinfeld to learn about Albee's delusions, since there is no mention of this issue prior to the conversation with Alzate. The revelation may create a sense of disorientation in the viewer that mirrors Albee's lived experience (does the viewer really know what is going on in this film?). When Albee is first introduced at the beginning of the film, she says that she has frequently been in and out of the Actors' Home and that she has just returned to it. At first, viewers may accept Albee's version of events as reality. However, at the midpoint of the film the viewer may doubt

Albee's earlier assertion. The viewer's confusion in watching the plot of the film (is Albee staying or leaving the production?) metatheatrically mirrors the residents' confusion regarding the plot of *A Midsummer Night's Dream* (why are these actors and fairies in the forest together?), which further metatheatrically mirrors the lived experience of disorientation that some of the neurodiverse residents of the assisted living facility have on a regular basis.

While Alzate is accustomed to working with neurodiverse people who experience delusions, Steinfeld is not. He ends the conversation by expressing the common stereotype about disability caregivers, conveying admiration for them and the sense that they do extraordinary work that requires special patience far beyond what 'normal' people have. It is common for those who do not have experience acting as disability caregivers to assume that such work is something that they could never do. While I would never want to underestimate the sacrifices made and the hardships experienced by some disability caregivers, an overestimation of what might be required in certain situations is also possible. Such overestimation may imply that someone with a disability is a 'burden' or may make some people feel that they would not be able to work with someone with a disability when they actually could. In terms of what this means for the production, Steinfeld is left feeling uncertain after his conversation with Alzate: 'Now I feel like we are in a slightly odd position. It is always great to talk to Yalile [Alzate] because she is the one who knows, who really knows, what is happening . . . I just feel like we are operating on nine or ten different realities in this room at any given time . . . I don't know what's harder; Gloria [Albee] telling me she's moving across the country tomorrow or finding out that she's not. I don't know what's harder to process.' Ultimately, Albee's belief that she will soon be moving makes it difficult to include her in regularly scheduled rehearsals.

During the rehearsals, the directors continue to point out themes from the play that may speak to the neurodiverse actors—for example, by drawing attention to passages that may parallel the failure of a shared sense of reality that often accompanies the experience of mental disability. In analysing the line, 'It seems to me / That yet we sleep, we dream' (4.1.192), Steinfeld draws parallels that clearly speak to Albee's experience of both memory impairment and delusions: 'In my opinion this is another version of just scrambling the world of our perceptions.

Did this thing happen? Well it happened for us because we saw it. But Bottom believes it was just a dream. How do we know if what we are experiencing is the real thing or the imagined thing . . . that's . . . .' A resident off camera helps Steinfeld to finish his thought by saying quietly, 'frightening'. Steinfeld agrees: 'incredibly frightening'. As the discussion ends, the camera focuses in on Albee's thoughtful facial expression. A disconcerting embellishment on the film's main melodic line follows in the music of the next scene, and the haunting minor key is accompanied by shots of the facility's hospital-like main corridor in which characters fade in and out like ghosts. Steinfeld's conclusion about how the directors should deal with Albee's delusions is to laugh loudly and move forward with humour: 'We'll just keep dealing with it. But I don't want to. I don't want to keep dealing with it. I would like to know what the fuck is going on.' Thus, Steinfeld acknowledges that trying to work with Albee and to understand her perspective is disorienting for him as a neurotypical director.

As the directors struggle to understand Albee's perspective, attempts to create collaborative work between the neurotypical directors and the neurodiverse residents result in serious communication difficulties. Perception becomes bound up with language and communication. As the two directors discuss the rehearsals over lunch, they are honest with each other about what they see as their lack of progress: 'If an audience just saw that, they wouldn't know what they were looking at . . . and the story is incomprehensible right now . . . A lot of the work that we have put in is clearly paying off—it just doesn't add up to them telling the story.' In order for words to have meaning, they have to have a shared referent. Mental disability often contributes to situations in which language and communication break down—in part because communication relies on speaker and listener having a shared frame of reference.[4] Disability studies scholar Margaret Price describes this as the problem of the 'mad rhetor': 'the failure to make sense, as measured against and by those with "normal" minds'.[5] As Price explains, 'social integration is key to narrative ability, which would seem to foreclose the possibility of a mad rhetor, for what is madness but a radical disunity of perception from that held by those who share one's social context?'[6] Furthermore, the English language is a neurotypical language—it does not have words for some neurodiverse experiences.[7] While the neurodiversity community has started creating words for perceptions for which there is no word in English, the process is slow and, in the meantime, much is lost in neurodiverse to neurotypical translation (and vice versa).

A lack of shared referent and different understandings of reality make it increasingly difficult for the directors to collaborate with Albee. In a later scene, when Albee says, 'I'm leaving the home', Steinfeld just nods understandingly and continues with rehearsal. But when Albee leaves the room, Brody says to Steinfeld, in a moment of confusion, 'Do you know what is happening right now?' Steinfeld responds to Brody with obvious bewilderment, 'Right now? No'. Albee refuses to return to rehearsal, explaining that she is busy packing: 'I'm packing in my room . . . I'm inundated in my room packing and stuff like that.' Steinfeld summarizes the situation with Albee, saying that it has been 'a couple of tough days with Gloria [Albee]. When she has bad days, she sequesters herself and apparently doesn't eat and doesn't drink. She's such a strong actor that it would be a big blow if we were to lose her.' It is unfortunate that no one at the home seems to wonder whether Albee's 'bad days' and repeated narratives of leaving might be a way for her to try to communicate that she wants to leave the home. Refusing to eat or drink is often a way in which patients passively attempt to resist unwanted medical care. In the end, Albee proves to be another actor who must withdraw from the production of *A Midsummer Night's Dream*, as increasing concerns about her health lead to her being transferred to a nursing facility.

While the neurotypical directors cope with trying to understand their actors' perceptions of reality and struggle to communicate with the actors clearly, they also find that they must grapple with differing perceptions of time. In other words, to successfully put on a production of Shakespeare's play, the able-bodied/neurotypical directors must learn to work in crip time. Crip time is the way in which disability and time interact with each other.[8] In its most common form, crip time is often taken to mean that people with disabilities may need more time to perform certain tasks (for example, someone with a mobility impairment may walk more slowly than an able-bodied person and thus take longer to arrive at his destination). However, not all people with disabilities experience crip time in the same way. For example, people with cognitive disabilities and their families have long noted that mental disability can fundamentally alter the perception of time.[9] For some people with mental disabilities, crip time is an acceleration, a speeding up rather than a slowing down—and sometimes, crip time is neither deceleration nor acceleration but, rather, a differing in the perception of what time is altogether. Time, and how we measure the passage of time, is a major focus in *Still Dreaming*. Early in the film, lines from *A Midsummer Night's Dream* about the moon and the measure of time ('Another moon—but O, methinks how slow / This old moon wanes! . . . Four days will quickly steep themselves in night, / Four nights will quickly dream away the time' (1.1.3–8)) echo in the background during a montage of shots depicting the daily goings-on of the assisted living facility. Scenes in the cafeteria are followed by views of hospital-style rooms, the nurses' station, and residents playing bingo. The sequence ends with a close-up of a pile of pamphlets stacked on a table that proclaim a *carpe diem* message: 'The time to be happy is now. The place to be happy is here.' There is a sort of stasis in the assisted living facility: for many of the residents, the same events happen every day—as though through repetition, they are frozen in time. As Steinfeld explains to Brody, 'One thing I'm starting to figure out is that the staff is comfortable with resetting every day.' Brody agrees: 'Sure. Because that's what they are used to.' However, this tendency to 'reset' every day as though the day before never happened leaves the neurotypical directors feeling frustrated. Steinfeld complains that 'I don't know how you build something that leads to a public performance like that. I want to feel like things are moving forward.' The need for a neurotypical sense of linear progress leaves the able-bodied directors frustrated with their neurodiverse actors, many of whom process information in a cyclical and repetitive way that relies on routine and sameness.

However, there are other ways in which crip time impacts life at the Actors' Home; *Still Dreaming* is a film not only about aging but also about how the experience of mental disability may change the perception of time. Some of the residents have memory impairments that make the past seem recent and that can cause more recent events to be quickly forgotten. This conflation of present and past, which in some cases becomes a replacement of the present with the past, is a part of how some of the residents experience crip time. O'Kelly remembers her days on the stage as the camera pans around walls full of playbills and framed production posters. Fairchild has conversations with her aide in which she reminisces about her work as a performer, stopping to demonstrate a few of her old dance steps. The actors make connections between the play and events in their lives when they were younger. For example, Lynette Loose, who plays Hermia, remembers that her marriage, at the age of 20, was not for love but, rather, to appease her parents: she uses those memories to relate to Hermia's situation at the beginning of the play. An air of nostalgia permeates the Actors' Home, and the film highlights this function of crip time by encouraging the actors to tell stories about the past and how they see that past as relating to the present. Indeed, the very act of putting on a play seems to invoke elements of the retired actors' earlier lives and younger selves.

The 'Magic' of Shakespeare: Cure versus Community

In setting Shakespeare up as the challenge that must be 'overcome', *Still Dreaming* follows some of the conventions of the heroic-overcomer narrative as well as replicating tropes that are common in metatheatrical films about Shakespeare in performance. Thus, the heroic-overcoming narrative of disability is combined with the familiar backstage narrative of the motley group of performers who come together and, just when the performance seems likely to fall apart, are transformed into actors by the 'magic' of Shakespeare.[10] In such backstage tales, viewers are inevitably meant to doubt whether the performers will be able to produce a good show, and *Still Dreaming* combines that familiar narrative arc with stereotypes about disability by using disability as the primary crux for suggesting doubt in the actors' abilities. Another facet of these kinds of backstage Shakespeare narratives is that what goes on before the performance must inevitably mirror the plot of the Shakespeare play performed. *Still Dreaming*, like *A Midsummer Night's Dream*, has a play within a play that in some ways reflects the larger plot of the story. Such parallels are humorously brought to light in the scene in which the directors must convince the unwilling Mary DePaulo to take the part of Quince:

> STEINFELD: There's a larger role that would be something more of a commitment on your part.
>
> DEPAULO: I don't know. I don't know what this is all about.

STEINFELD: This is the role of someone whose basically trying... she's like the director of a play, and she's trying desperately to keep it going... and basically she's got a bunch of unruly actors, kind of like... sort of like herding cats, if you know what I mean.

In the face of DePaulo's reluctance, the director explains that her role as Quince will be to direct the play within the play in *A Midsummer Night's Dream*, and that in doing so she will mirror Steinfeld, who is himself 'trying desperately to keep it [the show] going' and must deal with 'a bunch of unruly actors.'

Meanwhile, the film mirrors the ancient plot arc of traditional comedy, in which the younger generation comes into conflict with their elders. This conflict between the younger and the older generation comes to a climax during the final rehearsals, in which Dimo Condos dismisses the work of the two young directors. Condos argues that he should be in charge, 'because I have a lot of experience', and he refers to the two directors as 'children'. Losing his temper and yelling at everyone in the rehearsal room, Condos shouts at Steinfeld and Brody that 'You're not getting anything done and you know it', and he mocks their youthful hesitation by saying, 'I can do it better than you.' Although the young directors stand up to the more experienced actor and Condos eventually apologizes, the moment of tension parallels *A Midsummer Night Dream*'s larger thematic concern with a conflict between the expectations of the younger and the older generation.

While Shakespeare therapy may espouse Shakespeare as cure (see Chapter 3), *Still Dreaming* manages to uphold the mythology of Shakespeare being 'good for you' without sinking into the cure-based rhetoric that so many see as being antithetical to the disability rights movement. While the film may present participation in a Shakespeare play as beneficial for the inhabitants of the assisted living facility, it does not present Shakespeare as either therapy or cure. In keeping with the themes of *A Midsummer Night's Dream*, the film imagines Shakespeare as 'magic', while the two young directors make it clear that their intent is for the residents of the Actors' Home to enjoy themselves. The trailer for *Still Dreaming* begins with a montage of idyllic outdoor scenes while words appear slowly across the screen. These opening phrases promise the 'magic' of Shakespeare: 'There is a man who is creating magic... who is waking people up... reigniting dreams... His name is William Shakespeare.'[11] As with the Hunter Heartbeat Method (see Chapter 3), people with disabilities are imagined as metaphorically asleep, with Shakespeare being the force that can awaken them. In the trailer for the film, Shakespeare is associated with magic—with waking people up and with having dreams for the future all at the same time. The suggestion seems to be that people are asleep without art, without theatre, without Shakespeare. Aideen O'Kelly expresses this perspective in the film: 'The play [*A Midsummer Night's Dream*] is marvelous... It wakes people up. It truly wakes them up. It makes them think... instead of sitting all the time watching TV or playing Bingo, which I suppose is the most mindless game you could think of.'

From the beginning of the film, however, Steinfeld and Brody are clear that their intent is not to use Shakespeare as therapy. Rather, they try to bring these retired performers back to an activity in which they used to find great pleasure and joy. However, the Actors Fund administrators prove unable to escape the medical model in assessing the success of the project. The administrator of the Lillian Booth Actors' Home is interviewed at the end of the film, and he explains that 'We've actually been able to reduce some residents' medications. We've seen some residents who have a long history of depression and other psychiatric illnesses and all of a sudden it's like an awakening.' At the conclusion of the film, the directors also note some potential changes in Fairchild's memory impairment: 'Charlotte Fairchild seems to have retained, at least from this morning, maybe even from yesterday, some of the ideas that we are instilling about address to the audience and bringing her performance out and playfulness. She seems to have retained... which suggests some cumulative effect is taking place.' As Steinfeld explains this in a voice-over, the camera focuses in on Fairchild, who slyly says 'I remember' with clear joy. However, the medical-model interpretation that comes from the staff at the facility seems imposed—it comes only at the end of the film and is overshadowed by the comments of the residents.

The comments from the participants involved in the production reject the medical model: their feedback focuses on having fun, building self-esteem, and strengthening their sense of community. Fairchild says, 'That was fun'. Other participants say, 'I feel very happy', and 'I'm surprised at myself'. Loose concludes that 'This might be the best thing I've ever done. I discovered that I can feel good about myself. I loved it. I'm so glad that I did it.' The directors are pleased by the sense of general happiness the production brings to those living in the assisted living facility: 'From what the staff and administration say, it is having an impact on them and on just the home in general . . . there's this energy . . . and that's wonderful. That makes it worthwhile.' The focus here is on the community and the way in which the community at the assisted living facility benefits from the fun and excitement of the performance. Because family and friends from outside of the facility come to watch the show, it encourages those in the Actors' Home to connect both with each other and with the larger community outside the home. Although O'Kelly did not participate in the final performance, she feels that being involved in rehearsals helped to create a strong sense of community: 'The people in the cast were terrific people. If you fell down on your face, they would pick you up and carry you someplace. That's a feeling that you have. It's family. It's a real dream.' If Shakespeare has 'magic' in *Still Dreaming*, it turns out to be about having fun and building self-confidence. Perhaps even more importantly, the ending of the film turns the focus away from the cure of the medical model and toward using Shakespeare and performance as a means of strengthening disability community. This focus on community (rather than cure) puts *Still Dreaming*'s production of *A Midsummer Night's Dream* more in line with the social model of disability than the medical model and seems to foster a sense of inclusion among the residents of the assisted living facility.

In the end, *Still Dreaming* presents potential conflicts between neurotypical and neurodiverse conceptions of relationships, accommodations, sensory perceptions, and time, but it concludes by celebrating a potential union of neurotypical and neurodiverse perspectives as the directors and actors successfully work together to put on a Shakespeare play. Some of the tropes that emerge in the telling of this story are old and trite: the comic tension between the young and the old, the heroic overcoming of perceived challenges, the unlikely group of performers transformed by the power of Shakespeare. However, the film's focus on the cultural tensions that develop between the neurotypical directors and their neurodiverse actors is more unusual, and the happy resolution in which both parties learn from each other and come to work together, even more so. Ultimately, the film may serve to remind viewers that if Shakespeare's art has potential intellectual, emotional, or psychological benefits, such rough magic can be harnessed in ways that have nothing to do with therapy or cure.

Afterword

The Brilliant Red of Shakespeare

People are forever asking me, 'Why Shakespeare?' They think it will be a good conversation starter, I think—because I am so obviously obsessed with Shakespeare, and there must be a story there, a reason. In response, I always say (lightly, flippantly), 'you only live once'. Because to honestly answer the question 'Why Shakespeare?', I would have to say something about autism. I have often found that neurotypical interlocutors ask me about Shakespeare wanting to hear a neurotypical story (a story that they can relate to)—and when I'm being honest, that isn't always the kind of story I tell. Most autistic people have interests that are deeper and more intense than those of their neurotypical counterparts—in fact, 'special interests', as psychologists call them, have long been a part of the diagnostic criteria for autism spectrum disabilities. My special interest is in reading—I spend more time reading than anyone else I know. Both ultimate objective and near constant pastime, my deep interest in reading fundamentally defines my person, and since early childhood it has given me purpose. For me, this is a gift: my life is the single-minded and inevitable pursuit of the objective for which I was so obviously made. But to claim any particularly autistic pleasure is a tricky thing—many neurotypical people want to believe that their own interests are equally intense. Indeed, I have often found that some neurotypical people are not willing to acknowledge an autistic passion that might be outside of neurotypical experience, to believe that autism has its own pleasures.

Shakespeare and Disability Studies. Sonya Freeman Loftis, Oxford University Press (2021).
 DOI: 10.1093/oso/9780198864530.003.0006

In my mind, Shakespeare shows up as the most beautiful, brilliant red. It is a form of synaesthesia, this unexplained pairing of colours with concepts, which is more common in autistic people than in neurotypical people. I miss the brilliant red of Shakespeare when it isn't in my mind. I delight in the soothing blue of Milton, the royal purple of Toni Morrison, and the electric yellow of Bernard Shaw—but more than all the others I love the brilliant red of Shakespeare. Individual plays have their own distinct hues: *King Lear* is a bold blue, *Richard III* a rusty red, and *Hamlet* the deep brown of the earth. Lines are imbued with the shade of their source text, so that 'The weight of this sad time we must obey... Now is the winter of our discontent... O that this too too solid flesh would melt...' come through as a kaleidoscope of colour (*King Lear* 5.3.299, *Richard III* 1.1.1, *Hamlet* 1.2.129). The many colours of Shakespeare are beautiful to me, and this pleasure in synaesthesia is not a wrong or a lesser way to understand Shakespeare's text. It is a way to experience Shakespeare's work that is *different* from the perceived norm, a way to engage with literature that is specific to neurodiversity.

In this book, I have explored some of the ways in which disability, as cultural identity, lived reality, and aesthetic experience, may interact with the works of William Shakespeare. In doing so, I have tried to point out that our society's focus on disability as deficit, which implicitly affirms the medical model of disability, may sometimes lead Shakespearians to limit their possible readings of disability in Shakespeare. Thus, I have argued that while character-based readings (readings that examine Shakespearian characters as potentially representing disability in their fictional lives) are important and valuable, there are many other ways in which we can, and should, examine the potential intersections of Shakespeare studies and disability studies. Limiting Shakespeare and disability studies to character-based readings leaves Shakespearians symbolically bound to the medical model: such readings find disability within the individual character rather than in society at large. More importantly, such readings may turn focus away from the unique and aesthetic ways in which modern readers, scholars, and audience members with disabilities interact with Shakespeare's works.

The chapters in this book follow a progression from theory, through access, to inclusion. Creating 'inclusive Shakespeare', a version of

Shakespeare that opens up the text and performance of Shakespeare's works to as many readers and audience members as possible, is clearly an important goal from the standpoint of social equality and social justice. However, as I have argued in Chapter 3, inclusion is a goal that is difficult (perhaps impossible) to fully reach. Including people with disabilities in our classrooms and performances, thinking of their needs when we create and organize conferences, libraries, theatres, resources, and texts, means thinking about accessibility (Chapter 2) and striving for universal design (Chapter 3). Without accessibility, we will never reach real inclusion—and as I have argued throughout this book, meaningful, practical, and just access is rarely achieved without some knowledge of disability theory. At the very least, striving for access and inclusion means that we must reject compulsory able-bodiedness (Chapter 1) and recognize the presence of D/deaf, disabled, and neurodiverse lives and voices around us, that we must accept (dare I say 'embrace'?) the necessity of Shakespeare studies and disability studies being in dialogue with each other in the first place. In this way, theory (Chapter 1) leads to access (Chapter 2), and theory and access may help us to discover, understand, and create inclusion (Chapters 3 and 4). Indeed, using the insights of disability theory to create access is the only way we can be certain that our efforts at inclusion do not inadvertently become exclusion (Chapter 3).

There are many potential avenues for further work in Shakespeare and disability studies. More work needs to be done on modern performances that include actors with disabilities. (The challenges of making live theatre accessible to me means that I didn't write that book, although I will look forward to reading it when someone else does.) To date, very little work has been done in the field of Shakespeare studies on the intersectionality of disability with other identity categories such as race, gender, sexuality, and social class. Focusing on the lived experiences of people with disabilities rather than on literary characters may also open up the possibility of exploring biographical and autobiographical accounts of early modern people with disabilities (indeed, it is invigorating to see the work being done by Jonathan Hsy on the lived reality of medieval people with disabilities—and more of this same kind of work needs to be done for the Renaissance).[1] There needs to be further research on the engagement of students with disabilities with Shakespeare's text and on making Shakespeare classes and classrooms more accessible. Finally, there needs to be more work on early modern literature and disability studies written by scholars with disabilities, and we need to continue to fight for access and to strive for full inclusion for students and scholars with disabilities on our campuses, at our conferences, in our theatres, and in academia and the arts at large.

Disability studies is a critical lens that has been far too long neglected in Shakespeare studies. To dismiss disability studies in early modern scholarship as anachronistic does not do justice to crip theory as a complex and rich way of thinking about the world. I do not believe that the Shakespearian neglect of disability studies is a matter of simple ableism (although ableism could be a factor) but rather more likely a disregard born of misunderstanding. Embracing a disability studies methodology means doing more than just reading Shakespeare's plays through a certain theoretical lens—it should encourage us to do the social justice work that creates access and inclusion for modern people with disabilities in Shakespearian spaces. And think of all that we may miss if we do not achieve disability access—the diverse perspectives of other minds, the creative work of disability culture, the unique artistry of accommodation, and, most importantly, the unexpected joy of creating and experiencing real inclusion. We have diverse bodies, backgrounds, and brains, different sensory experiences and perceptions. What a shame it would be to exclude any seeking student or reader, any desiring performer or audience member, from having their own experience, in whatever form it might take for them, of the brilliant red of Shakespeare.

Notes

INTRODUCTION

1. For insights on reading disability in texts in ways that work outside of literary character see Michael Bérubé, *The Secret Life of Stories: From Don Quixote to Harry Potter, How Understanding Intellectual Disability Transforms the Way We Read* (New York: New York University Press, 2018).
2. David Houston Wood, 'Shakespeare and Disability Studies', *Literature Compass* 5, no. 8 (2011): pp. 280, 281; https://doi.org/10.1111/j.1741–4113.2011.00803.x.
3. Jeffery R. Wilson, 'The Trouble with Disability in Shakespeare Studies', *Disability Studies Quarterly* 37, no. 2 (2017); https://dsq-sds.org/article/view/5430/4644.
4. Americans with Disabilities Act of 1990, United States Department of Justice, Civil Rights Division, accessed 15 July 2019, http://www.ada.gov/ada_intro.htm.
5. Wood, 'Shakespeare and Disability Studies', p. 280.
6. See David T. Mitchell and Sharon L. Snyder, *Narrative Prosthesis: Disability and the Dependencies of Discourse* (Ann Arbor: University of Michigan Press, 2000), pp. 95–118. All of these examples (with the exceptions of blindness, madness, and obesity) are taken from a special issue of *Disability Studies Quarterly* 29, no. 4 (2009), 'Disabled Shakespeares', ed. Allison P. Hobgood and David Houston Wood; http://dsq-sds.org/article/view/991/1183. On early modern obesity as disability see Royce Best, 'Making Obesity Fat: Crip Estrangement in Shakespeare's Henry IV, Part 1', *Disability Studies Quarterly* 39, no. 4 (2019); https://dsq-sds.org/article/view/7149/5470.
7. Genevieve Love, *Early Modern Theatre and the Figure of Disability* (London: Bloomsbury, 2018) and Lindsey Row-Heyveld, *Dissembling Disability in Early Modern English Drama* (New York: Palgrave Macmillan, 2018).
8. See Ellen Samuels, 'My Body, My Closet: Invisible Disability and the Limits of Coming Out', in *The Disability Studies Reader*, ed. Lennard J. Davis, 4th ed. (New York: Routledge, 2013), Kindle edition, pp. 308–24.
9. Ellen Samuels, *Fantasies of Identification: Disability, Gender, Race* (New York: New York University Press, 2014).

10. Lennard J. Davis, 'Introduction: Disability, Normality, and Power', in *The Disability Studies Reader*, ed. Lennard J. Davis, 4th ed. (New York: Routledge, 2013), Kindle edition, pp. 1–2.
11. Wilson, 'The Trouble with Disability', *Disability Studies Quarterly.*
12. Wilson, 'The Trouble with Disability', *Disability Studies Quarterly.*
13. Elizabeth B. Bearden, *Monstrous Kinds: Body, Space, and Narrative in Renaissance Representations of Disability* (Ann Arbor: University of Michigan Press, 2019), Kindle edition, p. 7.
14. As Allison P. Hobgood and David Houston Wood point out in their collection *Recovering Disability in Early Modern England* (Columbus: Ohio State University Press, 2013).
15. 'Disability Impacts All of Us', Centers for Disease Control and Prevention, accessed 15 July 2019, https://www.cdc.gov/ncbddd/disabilityandhealth/infographic-disability-impacts-all.html.
16. For more on universal design see Margaret Price, *Mad at School: Rhetorics of Mental Disability and Academic Life* (Ann Arbor: University of Michigan Press, 2011), Kindle edition, ch. 2.
17. For further explanation of why it is impossible to achieve universal design, see Tom Shakespeare, *Disability Rights and Wrongs Revisited*, 2nd ed. (New York: Routledge, 2014), Kindle edition, pp. 36–46.
18. Matt Kozusko, 'Shakespeare and Civic Health', in *Disability, Health, and Happiness in the Shakespearean Body*, ed. Sujata Iyengar (New York: Routledge, 2015), p. 109.
19. Kozusko, 'Shakespeare and Civic Health', p. 114.
20. For more on the history of ableism, see David T. Mitchell and Sharon L. Snyder, *Cultural Locations of Disability* (Chicago: University of Chicago Press, 2006), pp. 3–36.
21. For further discussion of such colonial impulses in Shakespeare programmes, see Ayanna Thompson, *Passing Strange: Shakespeare, Race, and Contemporary America* (Oxford: Oxford University Press, 2011), pp. 138, 143, and Denise Albanese, *Extramural Shakespeare* (New York: Palgrave Macmillan, 2010), p. 128.
22. See Sheila T. Cavanagh, '"Denmark is a prison": *Hamlet* for Inclusive and Incarcerated Audiences', in *Shakespeare's Hamlet in an Era of Textual Exhaustion,* ed. Sonya Freeman Loftis, Allison Kellar, and Lisa Ulevich (New York: Routledge, 2018), pp. 103–18.

CHAPTER 1

1. In addition to a spine that showed an 80-degree curve caused by adolescent-onset scoliosis, the bones showed signs of arthritis that probably

caused frequent pain. See *Richard III: The New Evidence*, dir. Gary Johnstone, Darlow Smithson Productions, 2014. Where necessary, further references to *Richard III: The New Evidence* are noted parenthetically in the text. Thank you to Allison Kellar for bringing this documentary to my attention.

2. On the popular insistence that disability must be visible, see Ellen Samuels, 'My Body, My Closet: Invisible Disability and the Limits of Coming Out', in *The Disability Studies Reader*, ed. Lennard J. Davis, 4th ed. (New York: Routledge, 2013), Kindle edition, pp. 308–24.
3. Quoted in Lindsey Row-Heyveld, *Dissembling Disability in Early Modern English Drama* (New York: Palgrave Macmillan, 2018), p. 137.
4. David T. Mitchell and Sharon L. Snyder, *Narrative Prosthesis: Disability and the Dependencies of Discourse* (Ann Arbor: University of Michigan Press, 2000), p. 101.
5. Quoted in Mitchell and Snyder, *Narrative Prosthesis*, p. 101.
6. Mitchell and Snyder, *Narrative Prosthesis*, p. 101.
7. See David Bolt, *Metanarratives of Disability: Culture, Assumed Authority, and the Normative Social Order* (Routledge, forthcoming).
8. Quoted in Row-Heyveld, *Dissembling Disability*, p. 137.
9. Quoted in Row-Heyveld, *Dissembling Disability*, p. 162.
10. Abigail Elizabeth Comber, 'A Medieval King "Disabled" by an Early Modern Construct: A Contextual Examination of Richard III', in *Disability in the Middle Ages: Reconsiderations and Reverberations*, ed. Joshua Eyler (New York: Routledge, 2010), p. 189.
11. Comber, 'A Medieval King "Disabled"', p. 191.
12. Comber, 'A Medieval King "Disabled"', p. 188.
13. Row-Heyveld hints at this but does not use the term 'passing' (136).
14. Row-Heyveld, *Dissembling Disability*, p. 136.
15. Appleby quoted in Genevieve Love, *Early Modern Theatre and the Figure of Disability* (London: Bloomsbury, 2018), p. 191. I am fully aware of the irony of using this medical testimony in an effort to prove my point—but we live in a culture which often demands medical proof of disability.
16. Quoted in Love, *Early Modern Theatre*, p. 141.
17. David Houston Wood, 'Shakespeare and Disability Studies', *Literature Compass* 5, no. 8 (2011): pp. 280; https://doi.org/10.1111/j.1741–4113.2011.00803.x.
18. Lennard J. Davis, 'Introduction: Disability, Normality, and Power', in *The Disability Studies Reader*, ed. Lennard J. Davis, 4th ed. (New York: Routledge, 2013), Kindle edition, pp. 1–2.

19. Jeffery R. Wilson, 'The Trouble with Disability in Shakespeare Studies', *Disability Studies Quarterly* 37, no. 2 (2017); https://dsq-sds.org/article/view/5430/4644.
20. Wilson, 'The Trouble with Disability'.
21. Wilson, 'The Trouble with Disability'.
22. Wilson, 'The Trouble with Disability'.
23. Wilson, 'The Trouble with Disability'.
24. Wilson, 'The Trouble with Disability'.
25. Wilson, 'The Trouble with Disability'.
26. Robert McRuer, 'Compulsory Able-bodiedness and Queer/Disabled Existence', in *The Disability Studies Reader*, ed. Lennard J. Davis, 4th ed. (New York: Routledge, 2013), Kindle edition, pp. 361–71.
27. Robert McRuer, 'Fuck the Disabled: The Prequel', in *Shakesqueer: A Queer Companion to the Complete Works of Shakespeare*, ed. Madhavi Menon (Durham: Duke University Press, 2011), p. 296.
28. Denise Albanese, *Extramural Shakespeare* (New York: Palgrave Macmillan, 2010), p. 142.
29. Harold Bloom, *Shakespeare: The Invention of the Human* (New York: Riverhead Books, 1998).
30. 'Cripping up' is the term that disability theorists use to discuss the phenomenon of able-bodied actors feigning disability on stage. This is not to be confused with 'crip' theory or with 'cripping' the character of Richard III, which implies a commitment to rejecting compulsory able-bodiedness in literary criticism. For more on crip theory's resistance of compulsory able-bodiedness, see Robert McRuer, 'Fuck the Disabled: The Prequel', p. 296.
31. Tobin Siebers, 'Shakespeare Differently Disabled', in *The Oxford Handbook of Shakespeare and Embodiment*, ed. Valerie Traub (Oxford: Oxford University Press, 2016), p. 451.
32. McRuer, 'Fuck the Disabled', p. 295.
33. Row-Heyveld, *Dissembling Disability*, p. 136.
34. *Richard III: The New Evidence*, dir. Gary Johnstone, Darlow Smithson Productions, 2014.
35. Siebers, 'Shakespeare Differently Disabled', p. 443.
36. Ellen Samuels, *Fantasies of Identification: Disability, Gender, Race* (New York: New York University Press, 2014).
37. Row-Heyveld, *Dissembling Disability*, p. 2.
38. Siebers, 'Shakespeare Differently Disabled', p. 443.
39. *The Hollow Crown: The Wars of the Roses*, dir. Dominic Cooke, perf. Benedict Cumberbatch, Sophie Okonedo, Adrian Dunbar, Judi Dench, BBC, 2016. Unless otherwise noted, further citations and references throughout this section are from this work.

40. Mitchell and Snyder, *Narrative Prosthesis*, p. 96.
41. Mitchell and Snyder, *Narrative Prosthesis*, pp. 97–8.
42. See McRuer, 'Fuck the Disabled', p. 296.
43. See Row-Heyveld, *Dissembling Disability*, p. 141, and Katherine Schaap Williams, 'Enabling Richard: The Rhetoric of Disability in *Richard III*', *Disability Studies Quarterly* 29, no. 4 (2009), https://dsq-sds.org/article/view/997/1181.
44. Siebers, 'Shakespeare Differently Disabled', p. 436.
45. Love, *Early Modern Theatre*, pp. 144–5.
46. Row-Heyveld, *Dissembling Disability*, p. 144.
47. McRuer, 'Fuck the Disabled', p. 296.
48. McRuer, 'Fuck the Disabled', p. 296.
49. See Mitchell and Snyder, *Narrative Prosthesis*, p. 105; and Comber, 'A Medieval King "Disabled"', p. 194.

CHAPTER 2

1. 'Disability is an Art', UNSW Sydney: Newsroom, 21 October 2008, accessed 16 July 2020, https://newsroom.unsw.edu.au/news/social-affairs/disability-art.
2. 'About Shakespeare's Globe', Shakespeare's Globe, accessed 26 July 2019, https://www.shakespearesglobe.com/discover/about-us/.
3. 'Our Plan 2018–2020', Royal Shakespeare Company, accessed 26 July 2019, https://www.rsc.org.uk/about-us/policies/our-plan-2018–2022.
4. 'What is OSF?', Oregon Shakespeare Festival, accessed 26 July 2019, https://www.osfashland.org/en/company/mission-and-values.aspx.
5. 'Leadership Exchange in Arts and Disability', The Kennedy Center, accessed 26 July 2019, https://www.kennedy-center.org/education/networks-conferences-and-research/conferences-and-events/lead-conference.
6. David Bellwood, personal interview.
7. Josefa MacKinnon, personal interview.
8. Josefa MacKinnon, personal interview.
9. Josefa MacKinnon, personal interview.
10. Josefa MacKinnon, personal interview.
11. Josefa MacKinnon, personal interview.
12. Josefa MacKinnon, personal interview.
13. 'Sensory-Friendly Performances', The Kennedy Center, accessed 26 July 2019, https://www.kennedy-center.org/visit/accessibility/sensory/.
14. For more on this see Anne McGuire, *War on Autism: On the Cultural Logic of Normative Violence* (Ann Arbor: University of Michigan Press, 2016), Kindle edition, ch. 3.

15. 'Pre-Visit Stories', The Kennedy Center, accessed 26 July 2019, https://www.gettoknowthekc.org/stories/welcome#slide/beginning-of-the-show-20cb4534.
16. Josefa MacKinnon, personal interview.
17. Josefa MacKinnon, personal interview.
18. David Bellwood, personal interview.
19. David Bellwood, personal interview.
20. David Bellwood, personal interview.
21. Josefa MacKinnon, personal interview.
22. David Bellwood, personal interview.
23. Julie Simon, personal interview.
24. Josefa MacKinnon, personal interview.
25. Josefa MacKinnon, personal interview.
26. David Bellwood, personal interview.
27. David Bellwood, personal interview.
28. David Bellwood, personal interview.
29. David Bellwood, personal interview.
30. Julie Simon, personal interview.
31. David Bellwood, personal interview. As Bellwood explains, 'the Globe decided not to voiceover the Deaf actor playing that part. Though this would have provided "access" for people with no BSL, we felt it would have been an act of reduction and Deaf erasure. Bearing this in mind, we chose to add adapted voice over of Celia's lines in the live audio description . . . The patron in question dislikes audio description, and therefore chose to attend a non-assisted performance.'
32. 'Access', Royal Shakespeare Company, accessed 26 July 2019, https://www.rsc.org.uk/your-visit/access/.
33. Josefa MacKinnon, personal interview.
34. 'Access', Shakespeare's Globe, accessed 26 July 2019, https://www.shakespearesglobe.com/visit/access/.
35. If your programme wants a checklist for accessible theatre, the Kennedy Center has a list of resources at https://education.kennedy-center.org/education/accessibility/lead/resources.html.
36. Leah Lakshmi Piepzna-Samarasinha, *Care work: Dreaming Disability Justice* (Vancouver: Arsenal Pulp Press, 2018), p. 76.
37. Joanna Wood, 'Seeing Yourself for the First Time: the Power of People in Audio-Described Theatre', VocalEyes, accessed 26 July 2019, https://medium.com/@wearevocaleyes/seeing-yourself-for-the-first-time-the-power-of-people-in-audio-described-theatre-29e8c5b4d7c4.
38. Wood, 'Seeing Yourself for the First Time'.

39. Claire Szabo-Cassella, 'Oregon Shakespeare Festival', accessed 26 July 2019, https://redscooterdiaries.com/2018/08/08/oregon-shakespeare-festival/.
40. Mia Mingus, 'Access Intimacy: The Missing Link', *Leaving Evidence*, 5 May 2011, accessed 26 July 2019, https://leavingevidence.wordpress.com/2011/05/05/access-intimacy-the-missing-link/.
41. Szabo-Cassella, 'Oregon Shakespeare Festival'.
42. Mia Mingus, quoted in Kelsie Acton et al., 'Being in Relationship: Reflections on Dis-Performing, Hospitality, and Accessibility', *Canadian Theatre Review* 177 (Winter 2019).
43. Kelsie Acton et al., 'Being in Relationship'.
44. David Bellwood, personal interview.

CHAPTER 3

1. Alice Sheppard, Programme for *Descent*, Kinetic Light, Ferst Center for the Arts, 23 November 2019.
2. Drew Wiggins, 'Veterans Find a Path to Healing Through Shakespeare', *Mad in America: Science, Psychiatry, and Social Justice*, 13 October 2019, https://www.madinamerica.com/2019/10/veterans-find-path-to-healing-through-shakespeare/. Further citations and references throughout this section are from this work unless otherwise noted.
3. Kelly Hunter, *Shakespeare's Heartbeat: Drama games for children with autism* (New York: Routledge, 2015), Kindle edition, p. 5. Where necessary, further citations will be noted parenthetically in the text.
4. See Ayanna Thompson, *Passing Strange: Shakespeare, Race, and Contemporary America* (Oxford: Oxford University Press, 2011), p. 126.
5. Harold Bloom, *Shakespeare: The Invention of the Human* (New York: Riverhead Books, 1998).
6. I am not arguing that those who are incapable of communication, emotion, and/or play are not fully human—far from it. I am merely pointing out that various cultural stereotypes forward ableist definitions of the term 'human'.
7. See Nisonger Center, 'Shakespeare & Autism', The Ohio State University, http://nisonger.osu.edu/clinics-services/child/shakespeare-autism/, accessed 18 July 2017.
8. Nisonger Center, 'Shakespeare & Autism', n.p.
9. Nisonger Center, 'Shakespeare & Autism', n.p.
10. See Robin Post, 'Foreword', in *Shakespeare's Heartbeat: Drama games for children with autism* by Kelly Hunter (New York: Routledge, 2015), Kindle edition, n.p.

11. See Post, 'Foreword', n.p.
12. See Thompson, *Passing Strange*, p. 121; Michael P. Jensen, '"What service is here?": Exploring Service Shakespeare', *Borrowers and Lenders: The Journal of Shakespeare and Appropriation* 8, no. 2 (2013), http://www.borrowers.uga.edu/1039/show; Geoffrey Ridden, 'The Bard's speech: Making it Better; Shakespeare and therapy in film', *Borrowers and Lenders: The Journal of Shakespeare and Appropriation* 8, no. 2 (2013), http://www.borrowers.uga.edu/1015/show.
13. Matt Kozusko, 'Shakespeare and Civic Health', in *Disability, Health, and Happiness in the Shakespearean Body*, ed. Sujata Iyengar (New York: Routledge, 2015), p. 109.
14. Alan Sinfield, 'Give an account of Shakespeare and Education, showing why you think they are effective and what you have appreciated about them. Support your comments with precise references', in *Political Shakespeare*, ed. Jonathan Dollimore and Alan Sinfield (Manchester: Manchester University Press, 1985), p. 138.
15. Kozusko, 'Shakespeare and Civic Health', p. 114.
16. Sinfield, 'Shakespeare and Education', p. 136.
17. Kozusko, 'Shakespeare and Civic Health', p. 109.
18. Kozusko, 'Shakespeare and Civic Health', p.109.
19. Denise Albanese, *Extramural Shakespeare* (New York: Palgrave Macmillan, 2010), p. 142.
20. Ridden, 'The Bard's speech'; Thompson, *Passing Strange*, p. 121.
21. Marjorie Garber, 'Shakespeare as Fetish', in *Postmodern Shakespeare*, ed. Stephen Orgel and Sean Keilen (New York and London: Routledge, 1999), p. 243.
22. For further discussion, see Albanese, *Extramural Shakespeare*, p. 128, and Thompson, *Passing Strange*, pp. 138, 143.
23. Kozusko, 'Shakespeare and Civic Health', pp. 121–2; Thompson, *Passing Strange*, pp. 134, 143; Albanese, *Extramural Shakespeare*, pp. 138–9.
24. Ellen Samuels, 'My Body, My Closet: Invisible Disability and the Limits of Coming Out', in *The Disability Studies Reader*, ed. Lennard J. Davis, 4th ed. (New York: Routledge, 2013), Kindle edition, p. 313.
25. Swain and Cameron, quoted in Samuels, *The Disability Studies Reader*, p. 313; Garland-Thomson, quoted in Samuels, *The Disability Studies Reader*, p. 313.
26. Marc J. Tasse, 'Epilogue', in *Shakespeare's Heartbeat: Drama games for children with autism* by Kelly Hunter, (New York: Routledge, 2015), Kindle edition, p. 240.
27. Margaret H. Mehling, Marc J. Tasse, and Robin Root, 'Shakespeare and autism: an exploratory evaluation of the Hunter Heartbeat Method',

Research and Practice in Intellectual and Developmental Disabilities (2016), p. 12.

28. Mehling et. al., 'Shakespeare and autism', p. 10.
29. Post, 'Foreword', n.p.
30. Lila MacLellan, 'Autistic Kids are Thriving in Shakespearean Therapy', *Quartz*, 18 October 2016, https://qz.com/809771/autistic-kids-are-thriving-in-shakespearean-therapy-designed-by-a-british-actress-for-the-royal-shakespeare-company/.
31. MacLellan, 'Autistic Kids are Thriving', n.p.
32. Joseph N. Straus, 'Autism as Culture', in *The Disability Studies Reader*, ed. Lennard J. Davis, 4th ed. (New York: Routledge, 2013), Kindle edition, p. 457.
33. See Jim Sinclair, 'Autism Network International: The Development of a Community and Its Culture', in *Loud Hands: Autistic People, Speaking*, ed. Julia Bascom (Washington, DC: The Autistic Press, 2012), Kindle edition, p. 46.
34. Julia Bascom, 'The Obsessive Joy of Autism,' *Just Stimming* blog, accessed 26 July 2020, https://juststimming.wordpress.com/2011/04/05/the-obsessive-joy-of-autism/
35. Amanda Baggs, 'In my Language', YouTube video, 14 January 2007, https://www.youtube.com/watch?v=JnylM1hI2jc, accessed 18 July 2017.
36. See Nicola Shaughnessy's discussion in 'Curious Incidents: Pretend Play, Presence, and Performance Pedagogies in Encounters with Autism', in *Creativity and Community among Autism-Spectrum Youth*, ed. Peter Smagorinsky (New York: Palgrave Macmillan, 2016), pp. 187–216.
37. 'Red flags for autism', quoted in McGuire, *War on Autism*, n.p.; 'National Autistic Society Poster' quoted in Anne McGuire, *War on Autism: On the Cultural Logic of Normative Violence* (Ann Arbor: University of Michigan Press, 2016), Kindle edition. See also Shaughnessy, 'Curious Incidents', p. 191.
38. McGuire, *War on Autism*, n.p.
39. McGuire, *War on Autism*, n.p.
40. McGuire, *War on Autism*, n.p.

CHAPTER 4

1. *Still Dreaming*, dir. Hank Rogerson and Jilann Spitzmiller, Philomath Films, 2014. Unless otherwise noted, further citations and references throughout this chapter are from this work.
2. See, for example, Tom Shakespeare, *Disability Rights and Wrongs Revisited*, 2nd ed. (New York: Routledge, 2014), ch. 9.

3. Lennard J. Davis, 'The End of Identity Politics: On Disability as an Unstable Category', in *The Disability Studies Reader*, ed. Lennard J. Davis, 4th ed. (New York: Routledge, 2013), Kindle edition, p. 268.
4. Margaret Price, *Mad at School: Rhetorics of Mental Disability and Academic Life* (Ann Arbor: University of Michigan Press, 2011), Kindle Edition, ch. 1.
5. Price, *Mad at School*, Kindle Edition, ch. 1.
6. Price, *Mad at School*, Kindle Edition, ch. 1.
7. Ian Hacking, 'Autistic Autobiography', *Philosophical Transactions of the Royal Society B* 364 (2009), p. 1471.
8. Ellen Samuels, 'Six Ways of Looking at Crip Time', *Disability Studies Quarterly* 37, no. 3 (2017), https://dsq-sds.org/article/view/5824/4684.
9. See Michael Bérubé, *The Secret Life of Stories: From Don Quixote to Harry Potter, How Understanding Intellectual Disability Transforms the Way We Read* (New York: New York University Press, 2018), ch. 2.
10. For more on these kinds of backstage stories, see Matt Kozusko, 'Shakespeare and Civic Health', in *Disability, Health, and Happiness in the Shakespearean Body*, ed. Sujata Iyengar (New York: Routledge, 2015), p. 116.
11. *Still Dreaming* trailer, dir. Hank Rogerson and Jilann Spitzmiller, Philomath Films, 2014, https://stilldreamingmovie.com/.

AFTERWORD

1. Jonathan Hsy, 'Disability', in *The Cambridge Companion to the Body in Literature*, ed. David Hillman and Ulrika Maude (Cambridge: Cambridge University Press, 2015), pp. 24–40.

Further Reading

Disability Studies

Lennard J. Davis (ed.), *The Disability Studies Reader* (New York: Routledge, 2017, 5th ed.) is the place to begin for general background in disability studies: in addition to including essays that are classics in the field, this anthology also includes more recent chapters that represent new work that is being done in disability studies right now. The book is a useful starting point for scholars as well as for graduate students and advanced undergraduates. Davis's *The End of Normal: Identity in a Biocultural Era* (London: Verso, 1995) and *Bending over Backwards: Disability, Dismodernism, and Other Difficult Positions* (New York: New York University Press, 2002) are also seminal texts in the field and helpful for understanding the historical contextualization of the concept of the 'normal'. Sharon L. Snyder and David T. Mitchell's *Narrative Prosthesis: Disability and the Dependencies of Discourse* (Ann Arbor: University of Michigan Press, 2000) has become the single most important book for reading disability in works of literature and film. Their edited collection *Cultural Locations of Disability* (Chicago: University of Chicago Press, 2006) is also important: the book neatly lays out the contours of the field and includes some key essays that influenced the future direction of disability studies.

For more on disability theory, Tobin Siebers's *Disability Theory* (Ann Arbor: University of Michigan Press, 2008) is excellent, and for more on crip theory, Robert McRuer's *Crip Theory: Cultural Signs of Queerness and Disability* (New York: New York University Press, 2006) is the best place to begin. Rosemarie Garland Thomson's *Extraordinary Bodies: Figuring Physical Disability in American Culture and Literature* (New York: Columbia University Press, 1996) deals specifically with American literature, but it is a seminal text in the field of disability studies at large. Tom Shakespeare's *Disability Rights and Wrongs Revisited* (New York: Routledge, 2014) has also become a classic, offering a nuanced look at social justice issues and giving a complex critique of the social model of disability. Rachel Adams, Benjamin Reiss, and David Serlin (eds.), *Keywords for Disability Studies* (New York: New York University Press, 2015), is an extremely useful reference text: it has sustained and thoroughly researched entries on words ranging from 'Ability' to 'Accommodation,' from 'Freak' to 'Work', with many other important words relating to human embodiment and the disability rights movement in between. For analysing autobiographical approaches to disability, G. Thomas Couser's

Signifying Bodies: Disability in Contemporary Life Writing (Ann Arbor: University of Michigan Press, 2009) is the standard text. Ato Quayson's *Aesthetic Nervousness: Disability and the Crisis of Representation* (New York: Columbia University Press, 2007) focuses primarily on disability in modern works but has been influential in later readings of disability and literature.

The field of disability studies is diverse and highly interdisciplinary. More recent work that is shaping the direction of the field includes books focusing on a variety of disability identities—often those outside of physical disability, which was the primary focus of disability studies in its early years—or that combine crip theory with other theoretical approaches such as gender studies or critical race theory. On mental disability specifically, Margaret Price's *Mad at School: Rhetorics of Mental Disability and Academic Life* (Ann Arbor: University of Michigan Press, 2011) is an invaluable book for theorizing cognitive difference as it exists in and around academic spaces. Ellen Samuels's *Fantasies of Identification: Disability, Gender, Race* (New York: New York University Press, 2014) and Michael Bérubé's *The Secret Life of Stories: From Don Quixote to Harry Potter, How Understanding Intellectual Disability Transforms the Way We Read* (New York: New York University Press, 2016) are both recent books on 'invisible' disability that are having a significant impact on the field. For those interested in feminism as it intersects with disability, Alison Kafer's *Feminist, Queer, Crip* (Bloomington: Indiana University Press, 2013) is an excellent choice. Carrie Sandahl and Philip Auslander (eds.), *Bodies in Commotion: Disability and Performance* (Ann Arbor: University of Michigan Press, 2005) offers a strong collection of essays on disability, theatre, and performance. Sami Schalk's *Bodyminds Reimagined: (Dis)ability, Race, and Gender in Black Women's Speculative Fiction* (Durham: Duke University Press, 2018) brings together disability studies, critical race theory, and feminist theory.

Early Modern Disability Studies

Robert McRuer and David Bolt (eds.), *A Cultural History of Disability* (London: Bloomsbury, 2019), is useful for contextualizing diverse impairments in a variety of historical eras (the volumes in this series cover time periods ranging from classical antiquity to the modern era, and each volume includes chapters on different types of impairment such as 'atypical bodies' and 'mental health issues'). Particularly relevant for Shakespearians is the volume on the Renaissance: Susan Anderson and Liam Haydon (eds.), *A Cultural History of Disability in the Renaissance* (*A Cultural History of Disability*, Vol. 3, London: Bloomsbury, 2019). There have been three recent books on disability in Renaissance drama, all of them with a primary focus on character-based readings. Allison P. Hobgood and David Houston Wood (eds.), *Recovering*

Disability in Early Modern England (Columbus: Ohio State University Press, 2013), was the first major book on disability in Renaissance literature. The essays gathered in this collection deal with early modern subjects ranging from *Richard III* to the Book of Common Prayer, and they are bound together by an introduction that has a particularly modern and activist angle. Genevieve Love's *Early Modern Theatre and the Figure of Disability* (London: Bloomsbury, 2018) and Lindsey Row-Heyveld's *Dissembling Disability in Early Modern English Drama* (New York: Palgrave Macmillan, 2018) both focus primarily on non-Shakespearian Renaissance drama (although both include excellent chapters on *Richard III*). Love examines disability as textual metaphor, while Row-Heyveld is interested primarily in disability as performance and deception. Elizabeth B. Bearden's *Monstrous Kinds: Body, Space, and Narrative in Renaissance Representations of Disability* (Ann Arbor: University of Michigan Press, 2019) abandons character-based approaches to offer nuanced readings of early modern monstrosity in its potential to interact with disability theory, physical space, and narrative form.

At present, there has been more scholarship published on medieval disability than on disability in the Renaissance. Noteworthy work in medieval disability studies includes books such as Edward Wheatley's *Stumbling Blocks Before the Blind: Medieval Constructions of a Disability* (Ann Arbor, University of Michigan Press, 2010), Irina Metzler, *Disability in Medieval Europe: Thinking about Physical Impairment in the High Middle Ages, c.1100–c.1400* (New York: Routledge, 2006), and Joshua Eyler (ed.), *Disability in the Middle Ages: Reconsiderations and Reverberations* (New York: Routledge, 2010). A recent collection that combines medieval and Renaissance readings, Richard H. Godden and Asa Simon Mittman's (eds.) *Monstrosity, Disability, and the Posthuman in the Medieval and Early Modern World* (New York: Palgrave Macmillan, 2019), examines early modern disability primarily through the lens of mythologies of monstrosity. Jonathan Hsy's entry on 'Disability' in *The Cambridge Companion to the Body in Literature* (ed. David Hillman and Ulrika Maude, Cambridge: Cambridge University Press, 2015, pp. 24–40) combines embodied reality with literary texts by examining the autobiographical writing of a medieval deaf woman, Teresa de Cartagena, and bringing her work into conversation with fictional texts.

Shakespeare and Disability Studies

For those interested in early modern medicine, Sujata Iyengar's *Shakespeare's Medical Language: A Dictionary* (New York: Bloomsbury, 2014) is an excellent reference work—meticulously organized, Iyengar's dictionary offers detailed entries that neatly direct the reader to the relevant passages in Shakespeare while giving rich historical and medical background. Gail Kern Paster's

Humoring the Body: Emotions and the Shakespearean Stage (Chicago: University of Chicago Press, 2014) and *The Body Embarrassed: Drama and the Disciplines of Shame in Early Modern England* (Ithaca: Cornell University Press, 1993) both offer a focus on early modern embodiment and humoral theory that is outside of (but may lend a historical grounding to) early modern disability studies approaches. Allison P. Hobgood and David Houston Wood's special issue of *Disability Studies Quarterly*, 'Disabled Shakespeares' (2009), offers a collection of essays that read various Shakespearian characters through the lens of disability studies, including Katherine Schaap Williams's work on *Richard III* ('Enabling Richard: The Rhetoric of Disability in *Richard III*', *Disability Studies Quarterly*, vol. 29, no. 4, 2009) and Row-Heyveld's examination of disability and deception in *2 Henry VI* ('"The lying'st knave in Christendom": The Development of Disability in the False Miracle of St. Alban's', *Disability Studies Quarterly*, vol. 29, no. 4, 2009). Sujata Iyengar's (ed.), *Disability, Health, and Happiness in the Shakespearean Body* (New York: Routledge, 2015) combines health studies with disability studies, including a range of essays that move from a focus on early modern characters to a look at postmodern Shakespeare therapy.

Perhaps the two most defining articles in the field thus far are Tobin Siebers's 'Shakespeare Differently Disabled' (in *The Oxford Handbook of Shakespeare and Embodiment*, ed. Valerie Traub, Oxford: Oxford University Press, 2016, pp. 435–54) and Robert McRuer's 'Fuck the Disabled: The Prequel' (in *Shakesqueer: A Queer Companion to the Complete Works of Shakespeare*, ed. Madhavi Menon, Durham: Duke University Press, 2011, pp. 294–461). While Siebers applies his theory of 'complex embodiment' to disability in Shakespeare and thus reads Falstaff and Ophelia as disabled, McRuer offers a provocative reading of Ian McKellen's performance in Richard Loncraine's film of *Richard III*. *The Oxford Handbook of Shakespeare and Embodiment* includes a second chapter on disability alongside Siebers's: Vin Nardizzi's 'Disability Figures in Shakespeare' (ed. Valerie Traub, Oxford: Oxford University Press, 2016, pp. 455–68). *The Cambridge Guide to the Worlds of Shakespeare* also includes a chapter on disability in Shakespeare's works: Michael Schoenfeldt's 'Lessons from the Body: Moralizing Disability' (ed. Bruce R. Smith and Katherine Rowe, Cambridge: Cambridge University Press, 2016, pp. 795–802). Finally, David Houston Wood has written two articles that summarize the state of the field and raise possibilities for future work: 'Shakespeare and Disability Studies' (*Literature Compass*, vol. 8, issue 5, 2011, pp. 280–90) and 'Shakespeare and Variant Embodiment' (in *Shakespeare in Our Time: A Shakespeare Association of America Collection*, ed. Dympna Callaghan and Suzanne Gossett, London: Bloomsbury, 2016, pp. 189–93).

Index

For the benefit of digital users, indexed terms that span two pages (e.g., 52–53) may, on occasion, appear on only one of those pages.

www.ingramcontent.com/pod-product-compliance
Ingram Content Group UK Ltd.
Pitfield, Milton Keynes, MK11 3LW, UK
UKHW020417250726
13967UKWH00007B/2697